COOK'S COLLECTION

PASTA DISHES

Fuss-free and tasty recipe ideas for the modern cook

CONTENTS

···· ✕ ····

INTRODUCTION

Pasta Pronto! When we need something fast and delicious, more often than not we turn to a recipe using pasta. It's strange to think that a simple mixture of flour and water made into various shapes can be so popular across the world. Although plain cooked pasta doesn't have a distinctive taste, it is an excellent carrier for other flavours. That means the list of recipes is endless. Although we tend to think of pasta as being an Italian ingredient it has been adopted all over the world, with people from different culinary traditions putting their own spin on traditional recipes. In this book we've brought together savoury soups and sauces, hearty bakes, stuffed pasta and salads. There are vegetable-based recipes, meat, poultry and seafood too, all using one of the many pastas that are so readily available today. Some of the recipes will be familiar while others will be new and exciting and you'll just love to try them.

One of the great things about pasta is that it's dried and therefore a perfect storecupboard staple. Made from hard durum wheat, the ground flour is combined with water and sometimes egg and the dough is then extruded through heavy duty machines into a wide variety of shapes. After being dried it's ready to be packed and sent to your local supermarket.

It's good to have a selection of pasta on hand as different recipes cry out for their own special shape. Long spaghetti and tagliatelle, or wide pappardelle are great for chunky meat sauces such as Bolognese or for serving with meatballs. Layered dishes require flat lasagne sheets and ridged or twisted shapes cry out for creamy sauces that cling to the pasta and get trapped in the spirals and kinks. When you want to add pasta to a soup choose small shapes, and for salads, shells or spirals are perfect. There's also a rice-shaped pasta called orzo, popular in Mediterranean dishes, that can be added to a variety of dishes just before the end of the cooking time, or served on the side as an accompaniment.

Pasta made with wholemeal flour is more robust and has a nutty flavour and if your diet requires it, gluten-free pasta is also available, but always check the ingredients to ensure it's suitable for you. You can also buy fresh pasta which needs to be refrigerated or frozen, but it takes less time to cook than dried, so follow the cooking instructions on the packet. Look out for courgette and squash ribbons and vegetable lasagne sheets in the supermarket chilled section – they make a fresh alternative to wheat pasta. You can even make your own vegetable pasta if you purchase an inexpensive spiralizer.

Most children love pasta and the sauces served with them can be packed with goodness. Finely chopped vegetables will disappear when they're part of a slow-cooked tomato sauce, and when they're combined with familiar ingredients such as sausages, chicken and fish, no one will be any the wiser! Whatever pasta you choose for your recipe, you'll know you're cooking a healthy family favourite that won't fail to win their praise.

But don't be led to believe that pasta is just for mid-week, family meals. Some of the recipes in the book are great for entertaining, too. Creamy Turkey & Broccoli Gnocchi (page 74) is an excellent meal to feed a crowd, while Conchiglie with Balsamic-glazed Duck & Mushrooms (page 78) would make an impressive main course. By using pasta to bulk up the ingredients you won't need as much of the more expensive items for a really delicious dish. Pasta is perfect if you're feeding a crowd and many of the sauces can be prepared in advance and frozen. Whole dishes, such as Lasagne, can be prepared, frozen and baked when you need them – a great time-saver.

Cooking pasta is a breeze as all you need is a large, deep saucepan. Bring plenty of water to the boil – about 1.2 litres for every 125 g/4½ oz of pasta. The bubbling helps prevent the pasta sticking together. It's a good idea to add 1–2 teaspoons of salt, but this can be omitted if you're keeping your salt intake to a minimum. When the water is bubbling hard add small shapes of pasta in one go and stir well. Long pasta such as spaghetti should be fanned out slowly into the water as it softens, then stirred. Continue cooking the pasta, depending on the instructions, until tender but still firm to the bite. This is known as *al dente* in Italian. Cooking flat pasta such as lasagne sheets can be tricky and most recipes suggest using the no pre-cook variety, which is used dry, while using more liquid in the sauces to compensate.

Once the pasta is cooked, drain it in a colander and return to the saucepan – add a little oil if liked and stir well to help prevent the pasta sticking to itself. Serve immediately. If you're using the pasta for a salad, you need to drain it and then run cold water through the colander to prevent it overcooking. Pasta is best served freshly cooked although a lot of the sauces can be prepared ahead of time and reheated – the flavours in tomato-based sauces will intensify if left to stand for a while. When added to soup, pasta will continue to absorb liquid, so you may have to add a little stock or water when they're reheated.

If you're a real pasta person you may like the idea of making your own. The special pasta flour can be bought in supermarkets – just follow the instructions on the packet. You can roll out the pasta by hand and cut it into shapes or use a hand-cranked machine which will roll out the dough into strips – great if you want to make your own filled pasta, such as ravioli. You can also buy electric machines, which will do the mixing and extruding of the dough automatically. But when you get down to the basics, something that's to hand, ready-to-use and guarantees great results every time is best.

CHAPTER ONE

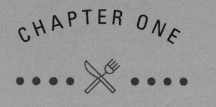

VEGETABLES

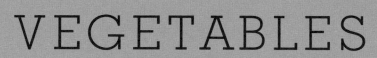

ROASTED TOMATO WHOLEWHEAT PASTA SALAD

SERVES: *4* | **PREP:** *10–15 mins* | **COOK:** *40–45 mins*

INGREDIENTS

600 g/1 lb 5 oz tomatoes in various colours and sizes, halved
2 garlic cloves, finely chopped
2 tbsp olive oil
225 g/8 oz dried wholewheat pasta, such as mafalda corta or quills
60 g/2¼ oz baby spinach
salt and pepper (optional)

SPINACH PESTO

50 g/1¾ oz fresh basil
25 g/1 oz baby spinach
25 g/1 oz pine nuts
25 g/1 oz freshly grated Parmesan cheese
4 tbsp olive oil
salt and pepper (optional)

1. Preheat the oven to 160°C/325°F/Gas Mark 3. Put the tomatoes in a roasting tin, cut side up, sprinkle with the garlic and the oil and season to taste with salt and pepper, if using. Roast in the preheated oven for 40–45 minutes, or until soft and just beginning to brown. Leave to cool, then chop up any larger tomatoes.

2. Meanwhile, add 1–2 teaspoons of salt, if using, to a large saucepan of water and bring to the boil. Add the pasta, bring back to the boil and cook for 10–12 minutes, or until just tender but still firm to the bite. Drain in a colander, rinse with cold water, then drain again.

3. To make the pesto, put all the ingredients in a blender and whizz until smooth. Lightly season with salt and pepper, if using.

4. Put the pasta and pesto in a salad bowl, toss together, then add the spinach and toss again briefly. Add the tomatoes and any pan juices, gently toss and serve.

VEGETABLE SOUP
WITH PISTOU SAUCE

SERVES: *4–6* | **PREP:** *20 mins* | **COOK:** *80 mins*

INGREDIENTS

500 g/1 lb 2 oz tomatoes, peeled,
deseeded and diced
85 g/3 oz French beans, cut into
bite-sized pieces
1 fennel bulb, quartered and sliced
1 carrot, diced
1 courgette, diced
1 bouquet garni of fresh flat-leaf
parsley, thyme sprigs and a
bay leaf
pinch of sugar
2 tbsp tomato purée
85 g/3 oz shelled broad beans or
85 g/3 oz shelled peas
400 g/14 oz canned haricot beans,
drained and rinsed
2 tbsp small dried soup pasta,
such as ditalini, or broken
spaghetti pieces
salt and pepper (optional)

PISTOU SAUCE

3 garlic cloves, roughly chopped
55 g/2 oz fresh basil leaves
25 g/1 oz freshly grated Parmesan
cheese, plus extra to serve
pinch of coarse sea salt
6 tbsp extra virgin olive oil, plus
extra to serve

1. Put the tomatoes, French beans, fennel, carrot, courgette, bouquet garni, sugar and tomato purée into a large, heavy-based saucepan. Pour in enough water to cover the vegetables by 7.5 cm/3 inches and generously season with salt and pepper, if using. Cover the pan and bring to the boil, then stir well, reduce the heat to very low and simmer for 40–45 minutes, or until the vegetables are very tender.

2. Meanwhile, to make the pistou sauce, crush the garlic in a large mortar. Add the basil, cheese and salt and grind together with the pestle until blended. Stir in the oil, tablespoon by tablespoon, then transfer to a bowl and set aside.

3. Uncover the soup and increase the heat to a slow boil. Add the broad beans and canned beans and boil for 5–10 minutes, or until the broad beans are tender. Add the pasta and boil for 3–5 minutes, or until the pasta is tender but still firm to the bite. The soup should be very chunky, but stir in extra water with the beans if too much liquid has evaporated.

4. Remove the bouquet garni. Stir in the pistou sauce. Taste and adjust the seasoning with salt and pepper, if using. Serve immediately with extra cheese and oil for adding at the table.

FRESH TOMATO SOUP
WITH PASTA

SERVES: *4* | **PREP:** *20 mins* | **COOK:** *1 hour 5 mins*

INGREDIENTS

1 tbsp olive oil
4 large plum tomatoes
1 onion, cut into quarters
1 garlic clove, thinly sliced
1 celery stick, coarsely chopped
500 ml/17 fl oz chicken stock
55 g/2 oz dried soup pasta
salt and pepper (optional)
4 tsp chopped fresh flat-leaf parsley,
*   to garnish*

1. Pour the oil into a large, heavy-based saucepan and add the tomatoes, onion, garlic and celery. Cover and cook over a low heat, occasionally shaking gently, for 45 minutes until pulpy.

2. Transfer the mixture to a food processor or blender and process to a smooth purée.

3. Push the purée through a sieve into a clean saucepan. Add the stock and bring to the boil. Add the pasta, bring back to the boil and cook for 8–10 minutes, or until the pasta is tender but still firm to the bite. Season to taste with salt and pepper, if using.

4. Ladle the soup into warmed bowls, sprinkle with chopped parsley and serve immediately.

ORZO &
VEGETABLE SOUP

SERVES: *2* | **PREP:** *5 mins* | **COOK:** *15–20 mins*

INGREDIENTS

1 tbsp olive oil

*1 bunch of spring onions, finely
    chopped*

900 ml/1½ pints vegetable stock

100 g/3½ oz dried orzo

*175 g/6 oz roasted red peppers,
    drained and sliced*

*100 g/3½ oz French beans, trimmed
    and cut into short lengths*

*85 g/3 oz spinach, stalks removed
    and leaves roughly chopped*

salt and pepper (optional)

*20 g/¾ oz Parmesan cheese
    shavings, to serve*

2 tsp extra virgin olive oil, to serve

1. Heat the oil in a saucepan over a medium–high heat, add the
spring onions and sauté for 2–3 minutes, or until starting to soften.

2. Add the stock and orzo and bring to the boil. Season to taste with
salt and pepper, if using, then cover and simmer for 8 minutes.

3. Add the red peppers, beans and spinach and cook for a further 2–3
minutes, then taste and adjust the seasoning, if necessary. Serve with
Parmesan cheese shavings and a drizzle of oil.

WHOLEMEAL LINGUINE WITH MARINATED TOFU

SERVES: 4 | **PREP:** 20 mins, plus marinating | **COOK:** 15 mins

INGREDIENTS

175 g/6 oz tofu, cut into cubes
   (drained weight)
350 g/12 oz wholemeal linguine
1 tbsp olive oil, for frying
125 g/4½ oz chestnut mushrooms,
   sliced
2 fresh thyme sprigs, leaves only
juice of ½ lemon
salt and pepper (optional)
2 tbsp chopped fresh parsley, to
   garnish
2 tbsp freshly grated Parmesan
   cheese, to garnish

MARINADE

1 tbsp olive oil
juice and zest of ½ lime
1 garlic clove, crushed
¼ tsp chilli flakes
2 tbsp soy sauce
2 tbsp clear honey

1. To make the marinade, mix all the marinade ingredients together in a large bowl. Add the tofu, making sure each piece is coated in the mixture. Leave to marinate for at least 30 minutes.

2. Cook the linguine according to the packet instructions.

3. Meanwhile, heat the oil in a frying pan, add the mushrooms and cook for 5–6 minutes over a medium heat. Toss in the thyme leaves and lemon juice just before removing from the heat.

4. Heat a griddle pan until hot, add the tofu and cook over a medium heat for 5–6 minutes until golden.

5. Drain the pasta and tip it into a large bowl with the mushroom mixture and the tofu. Season to taste with salt and pepper, if using. Toss together.

6. Serve the pasta garnished with chopped parsley and grated cheese.

COURGETTE SPAGHETTI

SERVES: *2* | **PREP:** *30 mins* | **COOK:** *25–30 mins*

INGREDIENTS

150 g/5½ oz cherry tomatoes
4 garlic cloves, sliced
1 tbsp olive oil
50 g/1¾ oz sunflower seeds
2 large courgettes
2 tbsp fresh pesto
70 g/2½ oz feta cheese, crumbled
salt and pepper (optional)
25 g/1 oz fresh basil, roughly
  chopped, to garnish

1. Preheat the oven to 200°C/400°F/Gas Mark 6. Cut half of the cherry tomatoes in half horizontally and leave the remainder whole. Place all the tomatoes and the garlic in a small roasting tin and drizzle over the oil. Shake well to coat and place in the preheated oven for 20 minutes.

2. Meanwhile, place a dry frying pan over a medium heat. Add the sunflower seeds and fry for 3–4 minutes, or until the seeds are just toasted. Set aside.

3. Lay a box grater on its side and grate the length of the courgettes into long strands. Try not to be firm – a loose grip makes this easier.

4. Bring a saucepan of water to the boil and add the courgette strips. Cook for 1–2 minutes, then drain thoroughly in a colander, gently squeezing away any excess water with the back of a spoon. Return the spaghetti to the pan and stir through the pesto. Season to taste with salt and pepper, if using.

5. Stir two thirds of the roasted tomato mixture, half of the sunflower seeds and half of the crumbled cheese into the spaghetti and divide the mixture between two plates. Top with the remaining tomatoes, sunflower seeds and cheese. Garnish with the basil and a sprinkling of pepper, if using. Serve immediately.

HOME-MADE SPINACH GNOCCHI WITH SLOW-ROASTED TOMATOES

SERVES: *4* | **PREP:** *35 mins, plus chilling* | **COOK:** *25 mins*

INGREDIENTS

400 g/14 oz cherry tomatoes
4 garlic cloves, finely sliced
1 tbsp fresh rosemary, roughly
  chopped
1 tbsp olive oil
1 tbsp fresh flat-leaf parsley, roughly
  chopped, to garnish

GNOCCHI

175 g/6 oz young spinach leaves
150 g/5½ oz ricotta cheese
100 g/3½ oz plain flour
2 eggs, beaten
100 g/3½ oz freshly grated
  Parmesan cheese
salt and pepper (optional)

1. To make the gnocchi mixture, bring a large saucepan of water to the boil. Plunge the spinach leaves into the water and wilt for 1 minute, then drain. Place the spinach in a clean tea towel and squeeze out as much liquid as possible from the leaves.

2. Finely chop the spinach and place in a medium bowl with the ricotta cheese, flour, eggs and Parmesan cheese. Mix well together, season to taste with salt and pepper, if using, and leave in the refrigerator for at least 1 hour, but preferably overnight.

3. Preheat the oven to 200°C/400°F/Gas Mark 6. Place the tomatoes on a baking tray with the garlic, rosemary and oil and roast in the preheated oven for 12–15 minutes until the skin on the tomatoes has blistered and they have begun to break down.

4. Meanwhile, using wet hands, shape the gnocchi mixture into 25 walnut-sized balls. Bring a large saucepan of water to a simmer and, using a slotted spoon, drop a few gnocchi into the water. Cook for 2 minutes before removing from the water, then keep warm in the roasted tomato tray while you cook the remaining gnocchi. Stir gently to combine.

5. Serve immediately garnished with fresh parsley.

TAGLIATELLE WITH ROASTED PUMPKIN & WALNUT PESTO

SERVES: *4* | **PREP:** *20 mins* | **COOK:** *25 mins*

INGREDIENTS

1 kg/2 lb 4 oz pumpkin or butternut
*   squash, deseeded, peeled and*
*   cut into 2-cm/¾-inch slices*
2 tbsp virgin olive oil
500 g/1 lb 2 oz fresh wholewheat
*   tagliatelle*
salt and pepper
*   (optional)*

WALNUT PESTO

85 g/3 oz walnuts, broken into
*   pieces*
6 tbsp virgin olive oil
15 g/½ oz fresh basil
25 g/1 oz thinly shaved Parmesan
*   cheese*
70 g/2½ oz rocket leaves

1. Preheat the oven to 200°C/400°F/Gas Mark 6. Arrange the pumpkin on a large baking sheet in a single layer. Drizzle with the oil and season to taste with salt and pepper, if using. Roast in the preheated oven for 20–25 minutes, or until just tender.

2. Meanwhile, to make the pesto, put the walnuts in a large frying pan and toast for 2–3 minutes, or until just beginning to brown. Transfer to a food processor or blender, pour in the oil and process until coarsely ground. Add the basil, cheese and half the rocket leaves and process again until you have a coarse pesto.

3. Add 1–2 teaspoons of salt, if using, to a large saucepan of water and bring to the boil. Add the tagliatelle and cook for 3–4 minutes, or until tender but still firm to the bite.

4. Drain the pasta and pour a little of the cooking water into a jug. Return the pasta to the pan. Cut the pumpkin into cubes and add to the pasta. Drizzle over the pesto and gently toss together, adding a little of the reserved pasta water if needed to loosen the sauce. Top with the remaining rocket, spoon into warmed bowls and serve.

BUTTERNUT SQUASH LINGUINE
WITH ARRABBIATA SAUCE

SERVES: *2* | **PREP:** *15 mins* | **COOK:** *20 mins*

INGREDIENTS

1 butternut squash

8 sprays cooking oil spray

2 tbsp chopped fresh flat-leaf parsley, to garnish

ARRABBIATA SAUCE

1 tbsp olive oil

1 onion, chopped

2 garlic cloves, crushed

1 red chilli, deseeded and finely chopped

3 tbsp red wine

1 tsp sugar

1 tsp chilli flakes

2 tsp red pesto

200 g/7 oz canned chopped tomatoes

4 anchovy fillets from a jar, drained

8 black olives, stoned and roughly chopped

1 tsp dried Italian seasoning

½ tsp salt

½ tsp pepper

1. Cut the bulbous end off the squash and set aside for use in another recipe. Peel the remaining squash. If you are using a spiralizer, cut the squash into two chunks and put each chunk through the spiralizer. If you are using a julienne peeler, sit the squash on a stable work surface and slice off julienne strips.

2. To make the arrabbiata sauce, place a large saucepan over a medium–low heat and add the oil. Add the onion and fry for 8 minutes, or until soft and transparent. Add the garlic and chilli and stir for 1 minute. Add the wine, sugar, chilli flakes, pesto, tomatoes, anchovies, olives, Italian seasoning, salt and pepper and simmer for 20 minutes.

3. Meanwhile, preheat the oven to 190°C/375°F/Gas Mark 5. Put the squash spaghetti on a large baking tray and spray with the cooking oil spray. Bake in the preheated oven for 6 minutes, then turn the spaghetti over using tongs. Bake for a further 4 minutes, or until the strands are just tender with the occasional tinge of gold.

4. Transfer the spaghetti to two warmed serving plates. Spoon the arrabbiata sauce over the spaghetti, garnish with the parsley and serve immediately.

WHOLEWHEAT SPAGHETTI WITH EDAMAME BEANS

SERVES: *4* | **PREP:** *5 mins* | **COOK:** *12–15 mins*

INGREDIENTS

350 g/12 oz wholewheat spaghetti

200 g/7 oz frozen edamame (soya) beans

2 tbsp extra virgin olive oil

2 garlic cloves, thinly sliced

finely grated rind of 1 lemon

salt and pepper (optional)

1. Add 1–2 teaspoons of salt, if using, to a large saucepan of water and bring to the boil. Add the spaghetti, bring back to the boil and cook for 10–12 minutes, or until tender but still firm to the bite. Add the edamame beans to the pan for the final 3 minutes of cooking. Drain well and keep warm in the pan.

2. Meanwhile, add the oil to a small frying pan over a low heat and stir in the garlic. Reduce to a very low heat so that the garlic can infuse for about 10 minutes, stirring occasionally, without allowing the garlic to sizzle or brown.

3. Add the lemon rind, garlic and oil to the spaghetti and beans and toss to combine evenly. Season to taste with salt and pepper, if using, and serve immediately.

KALE, LEMON & CHIVE LINGUINE

SERVES: *2–3* | **PREP:** *20 mins* | **COOK:** *20 mins*

INGREDIENTS

250 g/9 oz kale, thick stalks
removed, leaves sliced crossways
into thin ribbons
225 g/8 oz dried linguine
8 tbsp olive oil
1 onion, chopped
1 garlic clove, very thinly sliced
grated rind of 1 large lemon
large pinch of dried red chilli flakes
3 tbsp snipped fresh chives
4 tbsp freshly grated Parmesan
cheese
salt and pepper (optional)

1. Bring a large saucepan of water to the boil. Add the kale and blanch for 2 minutes until just wilted. Drain, reserving the water, and set aside.

2. Return the reserved water to the kale pan and bring to the boil. Add the linguine and cook for 10–12 minutes, or until tender but still firm to the bite.

3. Meanwhile, heat the oil in a large frying pan over a medium–high heat. Add the onion and fry for 2–3 minutes until translucent. Add the garlic and fry for a further 1 minute.

4. Stir in the kale, lemon rind and chilli flakes and season to taste with salt and pepper, if using. Cook over a medium heat for 4–5 minutes, stirring occasionally, until tender but still bright green in colour. Add a little of the cooking water if the mixture becomes dry.

5. Drain the pasta and tip into a warmed serving dish. Add the kale mixture, tossing with the pasta to mix. Stir in the chives and cheese with some salt and pepper to taste, if using. Toss the pasta again and serve immediately.

ORZO WITH MINT
& FRESH TOMATOES

SERVES: *4* | **PREP:** *20 mins* | **COOK:** *20 mins*

INGREDIENTS

350 g/12 oz orzo
125 g/4½ oz crème fraîche
150 g/5½ oz baby spinach
25 g/1 oz fresh mint, roughly
chopped
300 g/10½ oz cherry tomatoes,
roughly chopped
salt and pepper (optional)
1 tbsp roughly chopped fresh mint,
to garnish

1. Add 1–2 teaspoons of salt, if using, a large saucepan of water and bring to the boil. Drop the orzo into the water, stir vigorously to prevent the little grains sticking and then stir occasionally during cooking. Simmer for 8 minutes, or until the orzo is tender but still firm to the bite.

2. Drain the orzo, reserving 100 ml/3½ fl oz of the cooking water, and return to the pan with the reserved cooking water. Place the pan over a very gentle heat and add the crème fraîche and spinach. Stir until the spinach has wilted and the crème fraîche has coated the grains. Remove from the heat.

3. Stir in the mint and cherry tomatoes. Season to taste with salt and pepper, if using, garnish with mint and serve immediately.

SPAGHETTI WITH FRESH PEA PESTO & BROAD BEANS

SERVES: *4* | **PREP:** *25 mins, plus cooling* | **COOK:** *30–35 mins*

INGREDIENTS

250 g/9 oz broad beans
500 g/1 lb 2 oz dried spaghetti
salt and pepper (optional)

PEA PESTO

300 g/10½ oz peas
75 ml/2½ fl oz extra virgin olive oil
2 garlic cloves, crushed
100 g/3½ oz freshly grated
  Parmesan cheese, plus extra
  shavings, to serve
100 g/3½ oz blanched almonds,
  chopped
pinch of sugar
salt and pepper (optional)

1. To make the pesto, bring a saucepan of water to the boil. Add the peas, bring back to the boil and cook for 2–3 minutes until just tender. Drain and transfer to a blender or food processor.

2. Add the oil, garlic and cheese and process to a coarse paste. Add the almonds and process again. Add the sugar and season to taste with salt and pepper, if using. Set aside.

3. Add 1–2 teaspoons of salt, if using, to a saucepan of water and bring to the boil. Add the beans, bring back to the boil and cook until just tender. Drain and leave to cool, then peel off the dull skins.

4. Add 1–2 teaspoons of salt, if using, to a separate saucepan of water and bring to the boil. Add the spaghetti, bring back to the boil and cook for 8–10 minutes, or until tender but still firm to the bite. Drain, stir in the beans and toss with the pesto.

5. Turn out into a serving bowl, add a coarse grinding of pepper, if using, and serve immediately with cheese shavings scattered over the top.

MUSHROOMS WITH PASTA, PINE NUTS & PARMESAN

SERVES: *4* | **PREP:** *15 mins* | **COOK:** *20–25 mins*

INGREDIENTS

2 tbsp olive oil
25 g/1 oz butter
2 shallots, chopped
2 large garlic cloves, thinly sliced
450 g/1 lb chestnut or Portobello
   mushrooms, thickly sliced,
   halved if large
1 tsp marjoram
grated rind of 1 lemon
450 g/1 lb dried pappardelle or
   other wide ribbon pasta
75 g/2¾ oz pine nuts, toasted
300 ml/10 fl oz whipping cream
6 tbsp freshly grated Parmesan
   cheese, plus extra to serve
2 tbsp fresh flat-leaf parsley
salt and pepper (optional)

1. Heat the oil and butter together in a large frying pan. Add the shallots and fry over a medium heat for about 2 minutes until soft. Add the garlic to the pan and fry for a further 1–2 minutes until lightly coloured.

2. Add the mushrooms and marjoram to the pan. Increase the heat to medium–high and fry for 5–7 minutes, stirring, until the mushrooms start to release their liquid.

3. Sprinkle with the lemon rind. Season with salt and plenty of pepper, if using. Cook for a further 1–2 minutes, or until the liquid has evaporated.

4. Meanwhile, add 1–2 teaspoons of salt, if using, to a large saucepan of water and bring to the boil. Add the pasta and cook for 8–10 minutes, or until tender but still firm to the bite.

5. Add the pine nuts, cream and cheese to the mushrooms in the pan and stir until heated through.

6. Drain the pasta and tip into a large warmed serving dish. Pour the mushroom mixture over the top and sprinkle with the parsley.

7. Serve immediately with extra cheese for handing round.

RIGATONI WITH PEPPERS & GOAT'S CHEESE

SERVES: *4* | **PREP:** *15 mins* | **COOK:** *45 mins*

INGREDIENTS

2 tbsp olive oil

1 tbsp butter

1 small onion, finely chopped

4 red peppers, deseeded and cut
*   into squares*

3 garlic cloves, thinly sliced

450 g/1 lb dried rigatoni

125 g/4½ oz goat's cheese, crumbled

15 fresh basil leaves, shredded

10 black olives, stoned and sliced

salt and pepper (optional)

1. Heat the oil and butter in a large frying pan over a medium heat. Add the onion and cook until soft. Increase the heat to medium–high and add the red peppers and garlic. Cook for 12–15 minutes, stirring, until the peppers are tender but not mushy. Season to taste with salt and pepper, if using. Remove from the heat.

2. Add 1–2 teaspoons of salt, if using, to a large saucepan of water and bring to the boil. Add the pasta, bring back to the boil and cook for 8–10 minutes, or until tender but still firm to the bite. Drain and transfer to a warmed serving dish. Add the cheese and toss to mix.

3. Briefly reheat the sauce. Add the basil and olives. Pour over the pasta and toss well to mix. Serve immediately.

PASTA ALL' ARRABBIATA

SERVES: *4* | **PREP:** *20 mins* | **COOK:** *30 mins*

INGREDIENTS

150 ml/5 fl oz dry white wine
1 tbsp sun-dried tomato purée
2 fresh red chillies
2 garlic cloves, finely chopped
4 tbsp chopped fresh flat-leaf
   parsley
400 g/14 oz dried penne
4 tbsp fresh pecorino cheese
   shavings, to garnish
salt (optional)

SUGOCASA

5 tbsp extra virgin olive oil
450 g/1 lb plum tomatoes, chopped
salt and pepper (optional)

1. To make the sugocasa, heat the oil in a frying pan over a high heat until almost smoking. Add the tomatoes and cook, stirring frequently, for 2–3 minutes.

2. Reduce the heat to low and cook for about 20 minutes. Season to taste with salt and pepper, if using. Using a wooden spoon, press through a non-metallic sieve into a saucepan.

3. Add the wine, tomato purée, whole chillies and garlic to the pan and bring to the boil. Reduce the heat and gently simmer, then remove the chillies. Check and adjust the seasoning, if using, adding the chillies back in for a hotter sauce, then stir in half the parsley.

4. Meanwhile, add 1–2 teaspoons of salt, if using, to a large saucepan of water and bring to the boil. Add the pasta, bring back to the boil and cook for 8–10 minutes, or until tender but still firm to the bite. Add the sauce to the pasta and toss to coat.

5. Sprinkle with the remaining parsley, garnish with the cheese shavings and serve immediately.

PENNE WITH ASPARAGUS & BLUE CHEESE

SERVES: *4* | **PREP:** *10 mins* | **COOK:** *25 mins*

INGREDIENTS

450 g/1 lb asparagus spears
1 tbsp olive oil
225 g/8 oz blue cheese, crumbled
175 ml/6 fl oz double cream
350 g/12 oz dried penne
salt and pepper (optional)

1. Preheat the oven to 230°C/450°F/Gas Mark 8. Place the asparagus spears in a single layer in a shallow ovenproof dish. Sprinkle with the oil and season to taste with salt and pepper, if using. Turn to coat in the oil and seasoning. Roast in the preheated oven for 10–12 minutes until slightly browned and just tender. Set aside and keep warm.

2. Combine the cheese with the cream in a bowl. Season to taste with salt and pepper, if using.

3. Add 1–2 teaspoons of salt, if using, to a large saucepan of water and bring to the boil. Add the pasta, bring back to the boil and cook for 8–10 minutes until tender but still firm to the bite. Drain and transfer to a warmed serving dish, then add the asparagus and the cheese mixture. Toss well until the cheese has melted and the pasta is coated with the sauce. Serve immediately.

WILD MUSHROOM FUSILLI

SERVES: *4* | **PREP:** *15–20 mins* | **COOK:** *25–30 mins*

INGREDIENTS

400 g/14 oz dried fusilli

60 g/2¼ oz hazelnuts

4 tbsp olive oil

1 onion, chopped

4 garlic cloves, chopped

300 g/10½ oz mixed wild mushrooms (such as oyster or chestnut), roughly chopped

4 tbsp finely chopped fresh flat-leaf parsley

salt and pepper (optional)

1. Add 1–2 teaspoons of salt, if using, to a large saucepan of water and bring to the boil. Add the fusilli, bring back to the boil and cook for 10–12 minutes, or until tender but still firm to the bite.

2. Dry-roast the hazelnuts in a small, heavy-based frying pan for 3–4 minutes, or until the skins begin to brown. Turn them out of the pan onto a damp tea towel, fold the tea towel over the nuts and roll them on the work surface to remove most of the skins, then roughly chop the nuts.

3. Heat the oil in a large saucepan over a medium heat. Add the onion, garlic and mushrooms and fry for 5 minutes, or until beginning to brown. Stir in the chopped nuts and cook for a further 1 minute. Season to taste with salt and pepper, if using.

4. Drain the pasta and toss with the mushroom mixture and parsley to mix thoroughly. Serve immediately.

FUSILLI WITH COURGETTES & LEMON

SERVES: *4* | **PREP:** *15 mins* | **COOK:** *35–40 mins*

INGREDIENTS

6 tbsp olive oil

1 small onion, very thinly sliced

2 garlic cloves, very finely sliced

2 tbsp chopped fresh rosemary

1 tbsp chopped fresh flat-leaf parsley

450 g/1 lb courgettes, cut into 4-cm/1½-inch strips

finely grated rind of 1 lemon

450 g/1 lb dried fusilli

salt and pepper (optional)

4 tbsp freshly grated Parmesan cheese, to serve

1. Heat the oil in a large frying pan over a low–medium heat. Add the onion and gently cook, stirring occasionally, for about 10 minutes until golden.

2. Increase the heat to medium–high. Add the garlic, rosemary and parsley and cook for a few seconds, stirring.

3. Add the courgettes and lemon rind. Cook for 5–7 minutes, stirring occasionally, until just tender. Season to taste with salt and pepper, if using. Remove from the heat.

4. Add 1–2 teaspoons of salt, if using, to a large saucepan of water and bring to the boil. Add the pasta, bring back to the boil and cook for 8–10 minutes, or until tender but still firm to the bite. Drain the pasta and transfer to a warmed serving dish.

5. Briefly reheat the courgette sauce. Pour it over the pasta and toss well to mix. Sprinkle with the cheese and serve immediately.

SPAGHETTI
ALLA NORMA

SERVES: *4* | **PREP:** *20 mins* | **COOK:** *30 mins*

INGREDIENTS

175 ml/6 fl oz olive oil
500 g/1 lb 2 oz plum tomatoes,
  peeled and chopped
1 garlic clove, chopped
350 g/12 oz aubergines, diced
400 g/14 oz dried spaghetti
½ bunch fresh basil, torn
115 g/4 oz freshly grated pecorino
  cheese
salt and pepper (optional)

1. Heat 4 tablespoons of the oil in a large saucepan. Add the tomatoes and garlic, season to taste with salt and pepper, if using, cover and cook over a low heat, stirring occasionally, for 25 minutes.

2. Meanwhile, heat the remaining oil in a heavy-based frying pan. Add the aubergines and cook, stirring occasionally, for 5 minutes until evenly golden brown. Remove with a slotted spoon and drain on kitchen paper.

3. Add 1–2 teaspoons of salt, if using, to a large, heavy-based saucepan of water and bring to the boil. Add the pasta, bring back to the boil and cook for 8–10 minutes, or until tender but still firm to the bite.

4. Meanwhile, stir the drained aubergines into the pan of tomatoes.

5. Drain the pasta and place in a warmed serving dish. Add the tomato and aubergine mixture, basil and half the cheese. Toss well, sprinkle with the remaining cheese and serve immediately.

CHAPTER TWO

POULTRY

GRILLED CHICKEN & PESTO SALAD

SERVES: *4* | **PREP:** *15–20 mins* | **COOK:** *25–30 mins*

INGREDIENTS

4 large chicken thighs

2 tbsp sunflower oil or olive oil, for brushing

200 g/7 oz dried trifoli or fusilli pasta

200 g/7 oz fine French beans, chopped

300 g/10½ oz ready-made pesto, plus extra if needed

2 large tomatoes, sliced

salt and pepper (optional)

1 tbsp fresh basil leaves, to garnish

1. Preheat the grill to medium–high and position the grill rack about 7.5 cm/3 inches below the heat. Brush the chicken thighs with oil and season to taste with salt and pepper, if using. Brush the rack with a little oil, add the chicken thighs, skin-side up, and cook for 20–25 minutes, or until the chicken is cooked through and the juices run clear when a skewer is inserted into the thickest part of the meat. Remove from the heat and set aside.

2. Meanwhile, add 1–2 teaspoons of salt, if using, to a large saucepan of water and bring to the boil. Add the pasta, bring back to the boil and cook for 8–10 minutes, or until tender but still firm to the bite. Add the beans to the pan 5 minutes before the end of the cooking time.

3. Drain the pasta and beans, shaking off the excess water, and immediately tip into a large bowl. Add the pesto and stir until the pasta and beans are well coated. Set aside to cool.

4. When the chicken is cool enough to handle, remove the skin and bones and cut the flesh into bite-sized pieces. Stir into the pesto mixture and season to taste with salt and pepper, if using. Leave to cool completely, then cover and chill until required. (The salad will keep for up to 1 day, covered, in the refrigerator.)

5. Remove the salad from the refrigerator 10 minutes before serving. Arrange the tomato slices on a serving platter. Stir the salad and add extra pesto, if needed. Mound the salad on top of the tomatoes, garnish with basil leaves and serve immediately.

HONEY & MUSTARD
CHICKEN PASTA SALAD

SERVES: *4* | **PREP:** *25 mins* | **COOK:** *20 mins*

INGREDIENTS

250 g/9 oz dried fusilli
2 tbsp olive oil
1 onion, thinly sliced
1 garlic clove, crushed
4 skinless, boneless chicken breasts,
  thinly sliced
2 tbsp wholegrain mustard
2 tbsp clear honey
175 g/6 oz cherry tomatoes, halved
handful of mizuna or rocket leaves
salt (optional)

DRESSING

3 tbsp olive oil
1 tbsp sherry vinegar
2 tsp clear honey
1 tbsp fresh thyme leaves
salt and pepper (optional)

1. To make the dressing, put the oil, vinegar, honey and thyme into a small bowl with salt and pepper, to taste, if using, and whisk together until well blended.

2. Add 1–2 teaspoons of salt, if using, to a large saucepan of water and bring to the boil. Add the fusilli, bring back to the boil and cook for 8–10 minutes, or until just tender but still firm to the bite.

3. Meanwhile, heat the oil in a large frying pan. Add the onion and garlic and fry for 5 minutes. Add the chicken and cook, stirring frequently, for 3–4 minutes. Stir the mustard and honey into the pan and cook for a further 2–3 minutes until the chicken and onion are golden brown and sticky and the chicken is tender and cooked through and the juices run clear when a skewer is inserted into the thickest part of the meat.

4. Drain the pasta and transfer to a serving bowl. Pour over the dressing and toss well to combine. Stir in the chicken and onion and leave to cool.

5. Gently stir the tomatoes and mizuna into the pasta and serve.

CHICKEN PASTA SALAD
WITH WALNUTS

SERVES: *4–6* | **PREP:** *25 mins, plus standing* | **COOK:** *15 mins*

INGREDIENTS

115 g/4 oz egg pappardelle, broken
into 7.5-cm/3-inch lengths
coarsely grated zest of 1 lemon
2 tbsp extra virgin olive oil
4 carrots
2 courgettes
125 g/4½ oz cooked chicken, sliced
into thin strips
40 g/1½ oz walnut halves
5 tbsp snipped fresh chives
2 tsp white wine vinegar
3 tbsp walnut oil
salt and pepper (optional)

1. Add 1–2 teaspoons of salt, if using, to a large saucepan of water and bring to the boil. Add the pasta, bring back to the boil and cook for 8–10 minutes, or until tender but still firm to the bite. Drain thoroughly and tip into a serving bowl. Toss with the lemon zest, 1 tablespoon of the olive oil and season to taste with salt and pepper, if using.

2. Meanwhile, slice the carrots lengthways into thin strips, using a mandolin or very sharp knife. Trim the courgettes and remove a wide band of peel on opposite sides. Slice lengthways into thin strips, so that there is a narrow strip of green peel on each side. Put the carrots in a steamer and steam for 3 minutes, then add the courgettes and steam for a further 2 minutes until just tender.

3. Add the vegetables, chicken, walnuts and chives to the pasta, gently tossing to mix. Whisk the vinegar with ½ teaspoon of salt and ¼ teaspoon of pepper, if using. Whisk in the walnut oil and the remaining olive oil. Pour over the salad and toss again carefully. Leave to stand for 30 minutes to let the flavours develop. Serve at room temperature.

ITALIAN CHICKEN SOUP
WITH PARMESAN

SERVES: *4* | **PREP:** *20 mins* | **COOK:** *1 hour 10 mins*

INGREDIENTS

1 tbsp olive oil

350 g/12 oz boneless, skinless chicken thighs, diced

1 onion, chopped

2 garlic cloves, finely chopped

½ red pepper and ½ orange pepper, cored, deseeded and diced

450 g/1 lb tomatoes, peeled and chopped

750 ml/1¼ pints chicken stock

175 g/6 oz cauliflower

55 g/2 oz wholemeal spaghetti, broken into pieces

85 g/3 oz tenderstem broccoli

55 g/2 oz kale, shredded

25 g/1 oz freshly grated Parmesan cheese

salt and pepper (optional)

1. Heat the oil in a large saucepan, add the chicken and fry over a medium heat, stirring, for 5 minutes until just beginning to brown. Add the onion and cook, stirring, for 5 minutes until the onion is just beginning to colour.

2. Add the garlic, red pepper, orange pepper and tomatoes. Cook for 2 minutes, then pour in the stock and bring to the boil. Cover, reduce the heat and simmer for 40 minutes, stirring occasionally.

3. Cut the cauliflower into small florets and add to the pan with the spaghetti, broccoli and kale and simmer for 5 minutes until the spaghetti is tender but still firm to the bite. Add salt and pepper to taste, if using. Ladle into warmed bowls, top with the cheese and serve immediately.

CHICKEN SOUP WITH ANGEL HAIR PASTA

SERVES: *6* | **PREP:** *10 mins* | **COOK:** *40 mins*

INGREDIENTS

3 large eggs

3 tbsp water

*2 tbsp chopped fresh flat-leaf
  parsley*

*175 g/6 oz skinless, boneless
  chicken breast*

3 tbsp olive oil

1.5 litres/2½ pints chicken stock

115 g/4 oz dried angel hair pasta

salt and pepper (optional)

1. Preheat the grill. Lightly beat the eggs in a bowl with the water and a pinch of salt, if using, and stir in the parsley. Season the chicken with salt and pepper, if using, and brush with some of the oil. Grill for 4–5 minutes on each side, until cooked through and the juices run clear when a skewer is inserted into the thickest part of the meat, then remove from the heat and cut into thin strips.

2. Heat the remaining oil in a 20-cm/8-inch omelette pan, then add a quarter of the egg mixture, swirling the pan to spread it evenly. Cook over a medium–low heat until the underside is set, then flip over with a spatula and cook for a further few seconds. Slide the omelette out of the pan and set aside. Cook three more omelettes in the same way, then roll them up and cut them into thin slices to make threads.

3. Pour the stock into a large saucepan and bring to the boil. Add the pasta, breaking up the 'nests', bring back to the boil and cook for 5 minutes until tender but still firm to the bite. Add the chicken, season to taste with salt and pepper, if using, and cook for a further 3–5 minutes. Stir in the sliced omelette, remove from the heat and serve immediately.

TURMERIC CHICKEN WITH WHOLEGRAIN PASTA

SERVES: *4* | **PREP:** *15–18 mins, plus marinating* | **COOK:** *15 mins*

INGREDIENTS

650 g/1 lb 7 oz boneless, skinless
chicken breasts
225 g/8 oz wholewheat spaghetti
200 g/7 oz tenderstem broccoli,
stems thickly sliced
55g/2 oz walnut pieces, roughly
chopped
25 g/1 oz parsley, roughly chopped

TURMERIC GLAZE

2 tbsp virgin olive oil
1 tbsp wholegrain mustard
1 tbsp sherry or cider vinegar
1 tsp turmeric
2 tsp clear honey
2 garlic cloves, finely chopped
salt and pepper (optional)

1. To make the turmeric glaze, put the oil, mustard and vinegar into a small bowl, then stir in the turmeric, honey and garlic. Season with a little salt and pepper, if using.

2. Arrange the chicken breasts in a shallow rectangular non-metallic dish large enough to take them in a single layer. Spoon 2½ tablespoons of the glaze over both sides of the chicken, then cover the dish with clingfilm and marinate in the refrigerator for at least 30 minutes.

3. Preheat the grill and line the base of the grill pan with foil. Add the chicken, fold up the sides of the foil to make a dish and spoon over any remaining glaze from the china dish. Grill for 15–18 minutes, turning the chicken once or twice and spooning over the pan juices until brown, cooked through and the juices run clear when a skewer is inserted into the thickest part of the meat. Slice the chicken.

4. Meanwhile, add 1–2 teaspoons of salt, if using, to a large saucepan of water and bring to the boil. Add the spaghetti, bring back to the boil and cook for 5 minutes. Add the broccoli to a steamer and place over the spaghetti, cover and cook for 5 minutes until tender. Drain the spaghetti, reserving about 125 ml/4 fl oz of the cooking water. Return the spaghetti to the pan and add the broccoli.

5. Dry-fry the walnuts in a small frying pan until lightly toasted. Add to the spaghetti with the reserved glaze and pasta cooking water. Warm through, then sprinkle with the parsley. Spoon into bowls and arrange the chicken slices on top of the pasta. Serve immediately.

CHICKEN PEPERONATA BOWL

SERVES: *4* | **PREP:** *15 mins* | **COOK:** *35 mins*

INGREDIENTS

2 red peppers, deseeded and sliced

2 yellow peppers, deseeded and sliced

1 tbsp olive oil

2 red onions, peeled and finely sliced

300 g/10½ oz dried penne

4 skinless chicken breasts

2 garlic cloves, crushed

50 g/1¾ oz fresh basil

2 tbsp balsamic vinegar

2 tbsp fresh Parmesan cheese shavings

salt and pepper (optional)

1. Place the red peppers, yellow peppers and oil in a frying pan over a medium heat. Cover and cook gently for 15 minutes. Add the onions and cook for a further 15 minutes.

2. Meanwhile, add 1–2 teaspoons of salt, if using, to a large saucepan of water and bring to the boil. Add the penne and cook for 8–10 minutes, or until tender but still firm to the bite.

3. Preheat a griddle pan to hot, add the chicken breasts and cook them for 6–8 minutes on each side until cooked through.

4. Meanwhile, toss the garlic and basil in the pepper mixture, add the vinegar and cook for 2–3 minutes.

5. Drain the penne and toss into the peperonata. Season to taste with salt and pepper, if using.

6. Slice the chicken breasts diagonally. Divide the penne between four warmed bowls. Top with the chicken and some cheese shavings and serve immediately.

FETTUCCINE WITH CHICKEN & ONION CREAM SAUCE

SERVES: *4* | **PREP:** *20 mins* | **COOK:** *40 mins*

INGREDIENTS

1 tbsp olive oil

2 tbsp butter

1 garlic clove, very finely chopped

4 skinless, boneless chicken breasts

1 onion, finely chopped

1 chicken stock cube, crumbled

125 ml/4 fl oz water

300 ml/10 fl oz double cream

175 ml/6 fl oz milk

6 spring onions, diagonally sliced

35 g/1¼ oz freshly grated Parmesan cheese

450 g/1 lb dried fettuccine

salt and pepper (optional)

1 tbsp chopped fresh flat-leaf parsley, to garnish

1. Heat the oil and butter with the garlic in a large frying pan over a medium–low heat. Add the garlic and cook until just beginning to colour. Add the chicken and increase the heat to medium. Cook for 4–5 minutes on each side until cooked through and the juices run clear when a skewer is inserted into the thickest part of the meat. Season to taste with salt and pepper, if using. Remove from the heat and take the chicken out of the pan, leaving the oil in the pan. Slice the chicken diagonally into thin strips and set aside.

2. Reheat the oil in the pan. Add the onion and gently cook for 5 minutes until soft. Add the stock cube and the water, bring to the boil, then simmer over a medium–low heat for 10 minutes. Stir in the cream, milk, spring onions and cheese. Simmer until heated through and slightly thickened.

3. Meanwhile, add 1–2 teaspoons of salt, if using, to a large saucepan of water and bring to the boil. Add the pasta, bring back to the boil and cook for 8–10 minutes until tender but still firm to the bite. Drain and transfer to a warmed serving dish. Layer the chicken slices over the pasta. Pour over the sauce, garnish with the parsley and serve immediately.

FARFALLE WITH CHICKEN
& BROCCOLI

SERVES: *4* | **PREP:** *15–20 mins* | **COOK:** *25–30 mins*

INGREDIENTS

4 tbsp olive oil

5 tbsp butter

3 garlic cloves, very finely chopped

*450 g/1 lb skinless, boneless chicken
    breasts, diced*

¼ tsp dried chilli flakes

450 g/1 lb small broccoli florets

300 g/10½ oz dried farfalle

*175 g/6 oz bottled roasted red
    peppers, drained and diced*

250 ml/9 fl oz chicken stock

salt and pepper (optional)

1. Add 1–2 teaspoons of salt, if using, to a large saucepan of water
and bring to the boil. Meanwhile, heat the oil and butter in a large
frying pan over a medium–low heat, add the garlic and cook until
just beginning to colour.

2. Add the diced chicken, increase the heat to medium and cook
for 4–5 minutes until the chicken is cooked through. Add the chilli
flakes and season to taste with salt and pepper, if using. Remove
from the heat.

3. Plunge the broccoli into the boiling water and cook for 2 minutes.
Remove with a slotted spoon and set aside. Bring the water back
to the boil, add the pasta and cook for 8–10 minutes until tender
but still firm to the bite. Drain thoroughly and add to the chicken
mixture in the frying pan. Add the broccoli and roasted peppers.
Pour in the stock. Simmer briskly over a medium–high heat, stirring
frequently, until most of the liquid has been absorbed.

4. Transfer to warmed dishes and serve immediately.

FETTUCCINE WITH CHICKEN & BASIL PESTO

SERVES: *4* | **PREP:** *10–15 mins* | **COOK:** *10 mins*

INGREDIENTS

2 tbsp vegetable oil
4 skinless, boneless chicken breasts
350 g/12 oz dried fettuccine
salt and pepper (optional)
small handful of fresh basil, to
* garnish*

PESTO

100 g/3½ oz shredded fresh basil
125 ml/4 fl oz extra virgin olive oil
3 tbsp pine nuts
3 garlic cloves, crushed
55 g/2 oz freshly grated Parmesan
* cheese*
2 tbsp grated pecorino cheese
salt (optional)

1. To make the pesto, put the basil, olive oil, pine nuts, garlic and a generous pinch of salt, if using, in a food processor or blender and process until smooth. Transfer the mixture to a bowl and stir in the Parmesan cheese and pecorino cheese.

2. Heat the oil in a large frying pan over a medium heat. Add the chicken breasts and cook for 8–10 minutes, turning once, until the chicken is tender and the juices run clear when a skewer is inserted into the thickest part of the meat. Cut into small cubes.

3. Meanwhile, add 1–2 teaspoons of salt, if using, to a large saucepan of water and bring to the boil. Add the pasta, bring back to the boil and cook for 8–10 minutes, or until tender but still firm to the bite. Drain and transfer to a warmed serving dish. Add the chicken and pesto, season to taste with salt and pepper, if using, and mix together.

4. Transfer to warmed serving plates, garnish with basil and serve.

CHICKEN FETTUCCINE ALFREDO

SERVES: *4* | **PREP:** *20 mins* | **COOK:** *25 mins, plus standing*

INGREDIENTS

2 skinless, boneless chicken breasts
500 ml/17 fl oz chicken stock
475 ml/16 fl oz double cream
4 garlic cloves, very finely chopped
2 egg yolks
175 g/6 oz freshly grated Parmesan
*   cheese, plus extra to garnish*
25 g/1 oz chopped Italian parsley
450 g/1 lb dried fettuccine
salt and pepper (optional)

1. Put the chicken breasts and stock into a small saucepan and bring to a simmer over medium heat. Cover, reduce the heat to low and simmer for 12 minutes until the chicken is cooked through and the juices run clear when a skewer is inserted into the thickest part of the meat. Turn off the heat and leave the chicken in the hot stock for 15 minutes, then cut into thin slices and set aside.

2. Bring the stock back to the boil over a high heat and cook until the liquid has reduced by half. Add the cream and garlic and bring to a simmer, then reduce the heat to low.

3. Beat the eggs in a small bowl. Slowly whisk in a quarter of the hot cream mixture. Turn off the heat and whisk the egg mixture into the cream sauce. Stir in half the cheese and the parsley. Season to taste with salt and pepper, if using, and stir in the chicken.

4. Meanwhile, add 1–2 teaspoons of salt, if using, to a large saucepan of water and bring to the boil. Add the pasta, bring back to the boil and cook for 8–10 minutes until tender but still firm to the bite. Drain well, return to the pan and pour over the sauce. Stir well, cover, and leave to stand for 1 minute. Stir in the remaining cheese and leave to stand for a further 1 minute. Serve hot, topped with extra cheese to garnish.

LEMON CHICKEN COURGETTI

SERVES: *4* | **PREP:** *10 mins* | **COOK:** *8 mins*

INGREDIENTS

2 green courgettes

2 yellow courgettes

2½ tbsp olive oil

*2 large chicken breast fillets, cut
crossways into 10 slices*

1 tsp crushed coriander seeds

1 tsp crushed cumin seeds

½ tsp sea salt

½ tsp pepper

juice of 1 lemon

2 tbsp toasted pine nuts

3 tbsp fresh coriander leaves

1. Using a spiralizer, the side of a box grater or vegetable peeler, slice the courgettes into spirals or thin ribbons.

2. Add ½ tablespoon of the oil to a non-stick frying pan and place over a high heat. Add the chicken slices and fry for 1–2 minutes, or until lightly flecked with golden brown, turning once or twice. Reduce the heat to medium and add half of the remaining oil, the seeds, salt, pepper and half of the lemon juice.

3. Cook, stirring occasionally, for 5 minutes, or until the chicken slices are cooked through. Check that the centre of the chicken is no longer pink.

4. Meanwhile, heat the remaining oil in a separate large frying pan, add the courgette spirals and stir for 1–2 minutes, or until just tender and turning golden. Serve the chicken on the courgetti and scatter over the remaining lemon juice, pine nuts and coriander leaves.

CHICKEN RIGATONI
BOLOGNESE

SERVES: *6* | **PREP:** *15 mins* | **COOK:** *1 hour 15 mins, plus standing*

INGREDIENTS

3 tbsp olive oil

1 onion, chopped

900 g/2 lb fresh chicken mince

4 garlic cloves, finely chopped

2 tsp dried mixed herbs, to taste

90 ml/3 fl oz milk

*900 g/2 lb ready-made tomato
    pasta sauce*

*450 ml/15 fl oz water, plus extra if
    needed*

*handful of fresh flat-leaf parsley,
    chopped*

450 g/1 lb dried rigatoni

salt and pepper (optional)

*freshly grated Parmesan cheese, to
    serve*

1. Heat the oil in a large saucepan, add the onion and chicken and sauté over a medium heat for about 10 minutes, using a wooden spoon to break up the chicken, until the onion is soft. Add the garlic, herbs, salt and pepper to taste, if using, and milk. Cook, stirring constantly, for 2 minutes.

2. Add the pasta sauce, water and parsley and simmer, uncovered, over a medium–low heat for 1 hour until the chicken is cooked through. Add more water if needed to prevent the sauce becoming too thick.

3. Stir the pasta into the sauce, then remove from the heat. Cover and leave to stand for 2 minutes before serving with cheese.

SPAGHETTI WITH PARSLEY CHICKEN

SERVES: 4 | **PREP:** 15 mins | **COOK:** 35–40 mins

INGREDIENTS

1 tbsp olive oil

*thinly pared rind of 1 lemon, cut
  into julienne strips*

1 tsp finely chopped fresh ginger

1 tsp sugar

225 ml/8 fl oz chicken stock

250 g/9 oz dried spaghetti

55 g/2 oz butter

*225 g/8 oz skinless, boneless
  chicken breasts, diced*

1 red onion, finely chopped

*leaves from 2 bunches of flat-leaf
  parsley*

salt (optional)

1. Heat the oil in a heavy-based saucepan. Add the lemon rind and cook over a low heat, stirring frequently, for 5 minutes. Stir in the ginger and sugar, season to taste with salt, if using, and cook, stirring constantly, for a further 2 minutes. Pour in the stock, bring to the boil, then cook for 5 minutes, or until the liquid has reduced by half.

2. Meanwhile, add 1–2 teaspoons of salt, if using, to a large saucepan of water and bring to the boil. Add the pasta, bring back to the boil and cook for 8–10 minutes until tender but still firm to the bite.

3. Melt half the butter in a frying pan. Add the chicken and onion and cook, stirring frequently, for 5 minutes, or until cooked through and the juices run clear. Stir in the lemon and ginger mixture and cook for 1 minute. Stir in the parsley leaves and cook, stirring constantly, for a further 3 minutes.

4. Drain the pasta and transfer to a warmed serving dish, then add the remaining butter and toss well. Add the chicken sauce, toss again and serve immediately.

PASTA WITH HARISSA
TURKEY MEATBALLS

SERVES: *4* | **PREP:** *15 mins* | **COOK:** *20 mins*

INGREDIENTS

350 g/12 oz fresh turkey mince

55 g/2 oz dry breadcrumbs

6 tbsp Greek-style natural yogurt

1 egg

½ tsp ground coriander

½ tsp ground cumin

½–1 tsp harissa

3 tbsp finely chopped fresh parsley

*350 g/12 oz dried spaghetti or
    tagliatelle*

1 tbsp olive oil, for drizzling

salt and pepper (optional)

SAUCE

*400 g/14 oz canned chopped
    tomatoes*

*1 small chilli, deseeded and finely
    chopped*

¼ tsp ground cinnamon

½ tsp ground cumin

1. Preheat the oven to 200°C/400°F/Gas Mark 6. Line a baking sheet with baking paper.

2. Mix the turkey, breadcrumbs, yogurt, egg, coriander, cumin, harissa and parsley together in a bowl until thoroughly combined. Season to taste with salt and pepper, if using. Shape the mixture into golf ball-sized meatballs and put them on the prepared baking sheet. Bake in the preheated oven for 15 minutes until lightly browned.

3. Meanwhile, add 1–2 teaspoons of salt, if using, to a large saucepan of water and bring to the boil. Add the pasta, bring back to the boil and cook for 8–10 minutes until tender but still firm to the bite. Drain, transfer to a warmed dish, drizzle with the oil and toss to coat the pasta completely.

4. Meanwhile, to make the sauce, put all the ingredients into a saucepan and bring to a simmer. Cook, stirring occasionally, for 5 minutes until thickened.

5. Remove the meatballs from the oven and add to the pasta. Pour the sauce over them and toss together. Serve immediately.

TURKEY PASTA PESTO

SERVES: *4* | **PREP:** *10 mins* | **COOK:** *12 mins*

INGREDIENTS

150 g/5½ oz dried trofie or thin penne

100 g/3½ oz new potatoes, scrubbed and thinly sliced

100 g/3½ oz fine French beans, topped and tailed and cut about the same length as the pasta

2 tbsp olive oil

450 g/1 lb fresh turkey mince

2 large garlic cloves, crushed

150 g/5½ oz pesto sauce

salt and pepper (optional)

1. Add 1–2 teaspoons of salt, if using, to a large saucepan of water and bring to the boil. Add the pasta, bring back to the boil and cook for 12 minutes, or according to the packet instructions. Add the potatoes 7 minutes before the end of the cooking time, then add the beans 2 minutes later.

2. Meanwhile, heat the oil in a large frying pan over a medium–high heat. Add the turkey and fry, stirring with a wooden spoon to break it up into large clumps, for about 5 minutes until just starting to brown. Add the garlic and fry for a further 1 minute, or until the turkey is cooked through. Remove from the pan and keep warm.

3. When the pasta and vegetables are tender, drain, reserving a few tablespoons of the cooking water. Return the pasta and vegetables to the pan, add the turkey and pesto and toss together well. Add a little of the reserved cooking water, if necessary, and season to taste with salt and pepper, if using.

4. Divide the mixture between warmed bowls and serve immediately.

TURKEY
STROGANOFF

SERVES: *4* | **PREP:** *10 mins* | **COOK:** *25 mins*

INGREDIENTS

3 tbsp sunflower oil

450 g/1 lb fresh turkey mince

25 g/1 oz butter

1 onion, very finely chopped

*2 large garlic cloves, very finely
     chopped*

*250 g/9 oz chestnut mushrooms,
     trimmed and thinly chopped*

4 tsp Dijon mustard

pinch of freshly grated nutmeg

450 ml/15 fl oz soured cream

*1 tsp freshly squeezed lemon juice,
     or to taste*

900 g/2 lb cooked tagliatelle

salt and pepper (optional)

*4 tsp fresh flat-leaf parsley, roughly
     chopped, to serve*

1. Heat the oil in a large frying pan over a medium–high heat. Add
the turkey and fry, stirring with a wooden spoon to break up the
meat into large clumps, for 4–6 minutes until cooked through.
Remove from the pan with a slotted spoon and set aside.

2. Pour off all but 1 tablespoon of the fat remaining in the pan. Add
the butter and heat until melted. Add the onion and fry, stirring,
for 3–5 minutes until soft. Stir in the garlic and mushrooms and
season to taste with salt and pepper, if using. Fry, stirring, for about 5
minutes until the mushrooms re-absorb the liquid they give off.

3. Stir in the mustard and nutmeg, then return the turkey to the pan.
Stir in the soured cream and bring to the boil, stirring. Reduce the
heat and simmer for a few minutes until slightly reduced. Add the
lemon juice and adjust the seasoning to taste, if using.

4. Divide the pasta between four plates and pour over the sauce.
Sprinkle with parsley and serve immediately.

TURKEY TAGLIATELLE WITH LEMON PEPPER CREAM SAUCE

SERVES: *4* | **PREP:** *20–25 mins* | **COOK:** *30 mins*

INGREDIENTS

450 g/1 lb turkey steaks

grated zest of 1 lemon

2 tsp cracked black peppercorns

350 g/12 oz dried egg tagliatelle

1 tbsp olive oil

55 g/2 oz butter

juice of ½ lemon

250 ml/8½ fl oz double cream

4 tbsp chopped fresh flat-leaf
  parsley

salt (optional)

1. Place the turkey steaks between two sheets of clingfilm and flatten with a mallet. Slice the meat across the grain into thin strips measuring 1 x 9 cm/½ x 3½ inches. Put the strips in a shallow dish and toss with the lemon zest and the peppercorns.

2. Meanwhile, add 1–2 teaspoons of salt, if using, to a large saucepan of water and bring to the boil. Add the pasta, bring back to the boil and cook for 8–10 minutes, or until tender but still firm to the bite.

3. Heat the oil and half the butter in a saucepan, then add the turkey strips and fry for 5 minutes until no longer pink. Season to taste with salt, if using, then transfer to a plate and keep warm.

4. Add the remaining butter to the pan. Stir in the lemon juice and simmer for a few seconds. Pour in the cream, bring to the boil, then reduce the heat and simmer for 5 minutes, stirring frequently. Return the turkey to the pan, stirring until well coated with the cream.

5. Drain the pasta, reserving 4 tablespoons of the cooking water. Tip the pasta into a warmed serving dish. Stir the cooking water into the turkey mixture, then add the parsley. Pour the sauce over the pasta and toss to mix. Serve immediately.

CREAMY TURKEY & BROCCOLI GNOCCHI

SERVES: *4* | **PREP:** *15–20 mins* | **COOK:** *10 mins*

INGREDIENTS

1 tbsp sunflower oil

500 g/1 lb 2 oz turkey stir-fry strips

2 small leeks, sliced diagonally

500 g/1 lb 2 oz ready-made fresh gnocchi

200 g/7 oz broccoli, cut into bite-sized pieces

85 g/3 oz crème fraîche

1 tbsp wholegrain mustard

3 tbsp orange juice

salt and pepper (optional)

3 tbsp pine nuts, to serve

1. Heat the oil in a wok or large frying pan, then add the turkey and leeks and stir-fry over a high heat for 5–6 minutes.

2. Meanwhile, add 1–2 teaspoons of salt, if using, to a large saucepan of water and bring to the boil. Add the gnocchi and broccoli, bring back to the boil and cook for 3–4 minutes.

3. Drain the gnocchi and broccoli and stir into the turkey mixture.

4. Mix the crème fraîche, mustard and orange juice together in a small bowl. Season to taste with salt and pepper, if using, then stir into the wok.

5. Serve immediately, sprinkled with pine nuts.

TURKEY PASTA
PRIMAVERA

SERVES: *4* | **PREP:** *5 mins* | **COOK:** *35–40 mins*

INGREDIENTS

25 g/1 oz butter

2 tbsp olive oil

2 shallots, finely chopped

1 garlic clove, finely chopped

500 g/1 lb 2 oz diced turkey

115 g/4 oz asparagus tips

2 carrots, thinly sliced diagonally

115 g/4 oz mushrooms, thinly sliced

1 tbsp chopped fresh sage

*1 tbsp chopped fresh flat-leaf
    parsley*

150 ml/5 fl oz dry white wine

175 ml/6 fl oz double cream

*300 g/10½ oz dried pasta shapes,
    such as farfalle*

*55 g/2 oz freshly grated Parmesan
    cheese*

salt and pepper (optional)

1. Melt the butter with the oil in a large frying pan, add the shallots and garlic and cook over a low heat, stirring occasionally, for 3–4 minutes until soft. Add the turkey, increase the heat to medium and cook, stirring frequently, for 6–8 minutes until cooked through.

2. Add the asparagus tips, carrots and mushrooms and cook, gently stirring occasionally, for 4–5 minutes until starting to soften, then add the herbs, wine and cream. Reduce the heat and simmer, stirring occasionally, for 10–15 minutes until the vegetables are tender.

3. Meanwhile, add 1–2 teaspoons of salt, if using, to a large saucepan of water and bring to the boil. Add the pasta, bring back to the boil and cook for 8–10 minutes, until tender but still firm to the bite. Drain the pasta, tip it into the pan of sauce, season to taste with salt and pepper, if using, and toss well. Transfer to a warmed serving dish, sprinkle with the cheese and serve immediately.

CONCHIGLIE WITH BALSAMIC-GLAZED DUCK & MUSHROOMS

SERVES: *3–4* | **PREP:** *30 mins* | **COOK:** *1 hour 35 mins–1 hour 55 mins*

INGREDIENTS

4 duck legs, halved

125 ml/4 fl oz good-quality
balsamic vinegar

2 tbsp olive oil, for frying

1 onion, finely chopped

1 carrot, finely chopped

1 celery stick, finely chopped

1 large garlic clove, finely chopped

125 g/4½ oz chestnut mushrooms,
thinly sliced

400 ml/14 fl oz chicken stock

1 tbsp tomato purée

½ tsp dried oregano

squeeze of lemon juice

4 tbsp chopped fresh flat-leaf
parsley

350 g/12 oz dried conchiglie

salt and pepper (optional)

1. Remove the skin from the duck legs and discard. Place the joints in a frying pan and add the vinegar and bring to a simmer, turning the duck joints frequently for 10 minutes. Reduce the heat for 5 minutes, then remove the pan from the heat. Heat the oil in a saucepan and add the onion, carrot, celery and garlic and gently fry over a medium heat until soft but not coloured. Stir the mushrooms into the pan and cook for a further 5 minutes, then place the duck joints on top of the vegetables.

2. Pour the stock over the duck, then stir in the purée and oregano. Bring to the boil, then reduce the heat and simmer for 45–60 minutes, stirring occasionally, until the duck is tender.

3. Remove the duck from the pan with tongs and set aside tongs. Simmer the sauce for a few minutes until slightly thickened and reduced. Strip the duck meat from the bones, chop into small pieces and return to the pan. Add a squeeze of lemon juice and the parsley and season to taste with salt and pepper, if using. Gently simmer for 5 minutes.

4. Add 1–2 teaspoons of salt, if using, to a large saucepan of water and bring to the boil. Add the pasta, bring back to the boil and cook for 8–10 minutes, or until tender but still firm to the bite. Drain the pasta and transfer to a warmed serving dish. Add the sauce and toss, then serve immediately.

CHAPTER THREE

MEAT

BROAD BEAN, CHORIZO & PASTA SALAD

SERVES: *4–6* | **PREP:** *25 mins, plus standing* | **COOK:** *20–25 mins*

INGREDIENTS

225 g/8 oz dried pasta shapes, such as farfalle or fusilli

5 spring onions, some green included, sliced

250 g/9 oz shelled baby broad beans (frozen or fresh)

100 g/3½ oz chorizo, thinly sliced

6 tbsp extra virgin olive oil

2 shallots, finely chopped

2 tbsp red wine vinegar

2 tbsp chopped fresh thyme or marjoram

squeeze of lemon juice

¼ tsp dried chilli flakes

salt and pepper (optional)

1. Add 1–2 teaspoons of salt, if using, to a large saucepan of water and bring to the boil. Add the pasta, bring back to the boil and cook for 8–10 minutes, or until tender but still firm to the bite. Drain and transfer to a serving dish. Add the spring onions, tossing to mix.

2. Meanwhile, bring a separate saucepan of water to the boil, add the broad beans, bring back to the boil and cook for 4 minutes if frozen, 3 minutes if fresh. Drain under cold running water and pat dry with kitchen paper. Peel away the outer skins if they are tough, then mix the beans with the pasta and spring onions.

3. Cut the chorizo slices into quarters. Heat a large frying pan over a medium–high heat. Add the chorizo in a single layer and fry for 3–4 minutes until beginning to blacken slightly. Add to the pasta mixture and toss well.

4. Reduce the heat to medium–low and add the oil to the pan. Add the shallots and gently fry for 2 minutes until soft. Swirl in the vinegar and cook for a further few seconds. Tip the contents of the pan over the pasta mixture and toss to coat.

5. Stir in the herbs, lemon juice and chilli flakes and season to taste with salt and pepper, if using. Toss thoroughly to mix, leave to stand at room temperature for 30 minutes, then toss again and serve.

SPICY SAUSAGE SALAD

SERVES: *4* | **PREP:** *20 mins* | **COOK:** *35–40 mins*

INGREDIENTS

125 g/4½ oz dried conchiglie

2 tbsp olive oil

1 onion, chopped

2 garlic cloves, very finely chopped

*1 small yellow pepper, deseeded
    and cut into matchsticks*

*175 g/6 oz spicy pork sausage, such
    as chorizo, Italian pepperoni or
    salami, skinned and sliced*

2 tbsp red wine

1 tbsp red wine vinegar

125 g/4½ oz mixed salad leaves

salt (optional)

1. Add 1–2 teaspoons of salt, if using, to a large saucepan of water and bring to the boil. Add the pasta, bring back to the boil and cook for 8–10 minutes until tender but still firm to the bite. Drain thoroughly and set aside.

2. Heat the oil in a saucepan over a medium heat. Add the onion and cook until translucent. Stir in the garlic, yellow pepper and sausage and cook for about 3–4 minutes, stirring occasionally.

3. Add the wine, vinegar and pasta to the pan, stir and bring the mixture just to the boil over a medium heat.

4. Arrange the salad leaves on warmed serving plates, spoon over the warm sausage and pasta mixture and serve immediately.

MINESTRONE SOUP

SERVES: *4* | **PREP:** *20 mins* | **COOK:** *50 mins*

INGREDIENTS

2 tbsp olive oil
2 garlic cloves, chopped
2 red onions, chopped
75 g/2¾ oz Parma ham, sliced
1 red and 1 orange pepper,
*   deseeded and chopped*
400 g/14 oz canned chopped
*   tomatoes*
1 litre/1¾ pints vegetable stock
1 celery stick, chopped
400 g/14 oz canned borlotti beans
100 g/3½ oz cabbage, shredded
75 g/2¾ oz frozen peas, thawed
1 tbsp chopped fresh parsley
75 g/2¾ oz dried vermicelli pasta
salt and pepper (optional)
4 tbsp freshly grated Parmesan
*   cheese, to serve*

1. Heat the oil in a large saucepan. Add the garlic, onions and ham and cook over a medium heat, stirring, for 3 minutes, until slightly soft. Add the red pepper and orange pepper and the chopped tomatoes and cook for a further 2 minutes, stirring. Stir in the stock, then add the celery.

2. Rinse and drain the beans and add to the pan with the cabbage, peas and parsley. Season to taste with salt and pepper, if using. Bring to the boil, then reduce the heat and simmer for 30 minutes.

3. Add the pasta to the pan and cook for a further 8–10 minutes, or until tender but still firm to the bite. Remove from the heat and ladle into warmed bowls.

4. Sprinkle with the cheese and serve immediately.

MINCED BEEF
& PASTA SOUP

SERVES: *4* | **PREP:** *20 mins* | **COOK:** *50 mins*

INGREDIENTS

55 g/2 oz butter

2 tbsp olive oil

1 Spanish onion, finely chopped

1 garlic clove, finely chopped

450 g/1 lb fresh beef mince

1 tsp dried oregano

3 courgettes, thinly sliced

1.7 litres/3 pints beef stock

200 g/7 oz canned tomatoes,
*   drained and roughly chopped*

115 g/4 oz dried soup pasta, such
*   as stars and shells*

55 g/2 oz freshly grated Parmesan
*   cheese*

salt and pepper (optional)

1. Melt the butter with the oil in a large saucepan over a medium heat. Add the onion and garlic and cook, stirring occasionally, for 8 minutes until brown. Add the beef and cook, breaking it up with a wooden spoon, for 8–10 minutes until brown.

2. Sprinkle in the oregano, add the courgettes, pour in the stock and season to taste with salt and pepper, if using. Bring to the boil, then reduce the heat and simmer for 15 minutes.

3. Stir in the tomatoes and pasta and simmer for 5–8 minutes, or until the pasta is tender but still firm to the bite. Remove from the heat and pour into a warmed tureen. Sprinkle with the cheese and serve immediately.

ITALIAN SAUSAGE
& PASTA SOUP

SERVES: *4* | **PREP:** *25 mins* | **COOK:** *1 hour*

INGREDIENTS

2 tbsp olive oil

1 onion, chopped

1 carrot, chopped

1 celery stick, chopped

*450 g/1 lb Italian sausages, skinned
    and crumbled*

2 garlic cloves, finely chopped

2 bay leaves

½ tsp dried oregano

1 tsp crushed chillies (optional)

*400 g/14 oz canned chopped
    tomatoes*

900 ml/1½ pints chicken stock

*400 g/14 oz canned cannellini
    beans, drained*

*115 g/4 oz dried soup pasta, such
    as conchiglie*

*2 tbsp chopped fresh flat-leaf
    parsley*

salt and pepper (optional)

*25 g/1 oz freshly grated Parmesan
    cheese, to serve*

4 slices crusty bread, to serve

1. Heat the oil in a large saucepan, add the onion, carrot and celery and cook over a low heat, stirring occasionally, for 5 minutes. Stir in the crumbled sausages and garlic, increase the heat to medium and cook, stirring frequently, for a further few minutes until the meat is brown all over.

2. Add the bay leaves, oregano, crushed chillies, if using, tomatoes and stock and bring to the boil, stirring frequently. Reduce the heat, partially cover and simmer for 30 minutes.

3. Stir in the beans and pasta and simmer for a further 5–8 minutes, or until the pasta is tender but still firm to the bite. Season to taste with salt and pepper, if using, stir in the parsley and remove from the heat. Remove and discard the bay leaves, ladle the soup into warmed mugs or bowls and serve immediately with the cheese and bread.

SPAGHETTI
& MEATBALLS

SERVES: *4* | **PREP:** *25–30 mins* | **COOK:** *50 mins*

INGREDIENTS

*50 g/1¾ oz fresh white
    breadcrumbs*
50 ml/1¾ fl oz skimmed milk
400 g/14 oz fresh lean pork mince
1 onion, very finely chopped
2 garlic cloves, crushed
2 tbsp chopped fresh parsley
2 tsp crushed fennel seeds
1 tbsp olive oil
*300 g/10½ oz dried wholegrain
    spelt spaghetti, or wholemeal
    spaghetti*
salt and pepper (optional)
fresh basil leaves, to garnish

SAUCE

*125 g/4½ oz courgettes, coarsely
    grated*
3 garlic cloves, finely grated
*800 g/1 lb 12 oz canned chopped
    tomatoes*
1 tbsp tomato purée
1 tsp maple syrup
1 tsp red wine vinegar

1. Mix the breadcrumbs with the milk and leave to soak for a few minutes, then transfer to a mixing bowl and add the pork, onion, garlic, parsley, fennel seeds, and a little salt and pepper, if using. Combine well, then shape into 16 meatballs, transferring each to a plate as you shape it.

2. Heat the oil in a large frying pan with a lid. Add the meatballs and cook, uncovered, over a medium–high heat for a few minutes, turning occasionally, until slightly brown all over. Transfer to a plate with a slotted spoon, cover and set aside.

3. To make the sauce, reduce the heat to medium and add the courgettes to the pan. Cook for 1–2 minutes, then add the garlic and cook for a few seconds.

4. Add the tomatoes, tomato purée, maple syrup and vinegar, mix thoroughly and bring to a gentle simmer. Cover and cook for 15 minutes, then remove the lid and cook, stirring occasionally, for a further 10 minutes.

5. Return the meatballs to the pan and stir to coat in the sauce, then cook for a further 10 minutes, or until about half the liquid has evaporated and you have a rich sauce.

6. Meanwhile, add 1–2 teaspoons of salt, if using, to a large saucepan of water and bring to the boil. Add the spaghetti , bring back to the boil and cook for 8–10 minutes, or until tender but still firm to the bite. Drain, transfer to a serving platter and spoon the tomato sauce and meatballs on top. Garnish with basil leaves and serve immediately.

SPAGHETTI BOLOGNESE

SERVES: *4* | **PREP:** *25 mins* | **COOK:** *1 hour*

INGREDIENTS

1 tbsp olive oil

1 onion, finely chopped

2 garlic cloves, chopped

1 carrot, chopped

1 celery stick, chopped

*50 g/1¾ oz pancetta or streaky
  bacon, diced*

350 g/12 oz fresh beef mince

*400 g/14 oz canned chopped
  tomatoes*

2 tsp dried oregano

125 ml/4 fl oz red wine

2 tbsp tomato purée

350 g/12 oz dried spaghetti

salt and pepper (optional)

*1 tbsp chopped fresh flat-leaf
  parsley, to garnish*

1. Heat the oil in a large frying pan. Add the onion and cook for 3 minutes. Add the garlic, carrot, celery and pancetta and sauté for 3–4 minutes, or until just beginning to brown.

2. Add the beef and cook over a high heat for a further 3 minutes, or until brown all over. Stir in the tomatoes, oregano and red wine and bring to the boil. Reduce the heat and simmer for about 45 minutes.

3. Stir in the tomato purée and season to taste with salt and pepper, if using.

4. Add 1–2 teaspoons of salt, if using, to a large saucepan of water and bring to the boil. Add the spaghetti, bring back to the boil and cook for 8–10 minutes, or until tender but still firm to the bite. Drain.

5. Transfer the spaghetti to warmed serving plates and pour over the sauce. Toss to combine the pasta and sauce, garnish with the parsley and serve immediately.

TAGLIATELLE WITH
A RICH MEAT SAUCE

SERVES: *4* | **PREP:** *20 mins* | **COOK:** *55 mins–1 hour*

INGREDIENTS

5 tbsp olive oil
85 g/3 oz pancetta, diced
1 onion, chopped
1 garlic clove, finely chopped
1 carrot, chopped
1 celery stick, chopped
225 g/8 oz fresh beef mince
115 g/4 oz chicken livers
2 tbsp passata
125 ml/4 fl oz dry white wine
225 ml/8 fl oz beef stock
1 tbsp chopped fresh oregano
1 bay leaf
450 g/1 lb dried tagliatelle
salt and pepper (optional)
*freshly grated Parmesan cheese, to
   serve*

1. Heat 4 tablespoons of the oil in a large heavy-based saucepan. Add the pancetta and cook over a medium heat, stirring occasionally, for 3–5 minutes until it is just turning brown.

2. Add the onion, garlic, carrot and celery and cook, stirring occasionally, for a further 5 minutes.

3. Add the beef and cook over a high heat, breaking up the meat with a wooden spoon, for 5 minutes until brown.

4. Stir in the chicken livers and cook, stirring occasionally, for a further 2–3 minutes.

5. Add the passata, wine, stock, oregano and bay leaf and season to taste with salt and pepper, if using. Bring to the boil, reduce the heat, then cover and simmer for 30–35 minutes.

6. Meanwhile, add 1–2 teaspoons of salt, if using, to a large saucepan of water and bring to the boil. Add the pasta, bring back to the boil and cook for 8–10 minutes, or until tender but still firm to the bite.

7. Drain the pasta and transfer to a warmed serving dish. Drizzle with the remaining oil and toss well.

8. Remove and discard the bay leaf from the sauce, then pour the sauce over the pasta, toss again and serve with the cheese.

PASTA WITH BEEF ROLLS

SERVES: *4* | **PREP:** *45 mins* | **COOK:** *40–45 mins*

INGREDIENTS

2 garlic cloves

4 x 150-g/5½-oz very thin slices of lean beef

8 celery leaves

55 g/2 oz freshly grated Parmesan cheese

2 tsp capers, rinsed

4 tbsp olive oil

55 g/2 oz pancetta, diced

1 kg/2 lb 4 oz ripe plum tomatoes, peeled and chopped

400 g/14 oz dried orecchiette

salt and pepper (optional)

1. Finely chop 1 garlic clove and peel the other. Spread out the slices of beef on a work surface and season to taste with salt and pepper, if using. Place two celery leaves in the centre of each slice and scatter over the chopped garlic. Sprinkle with ½ teaspoon of the cheese and divide the capers between the beef slices. Roll up each slice like a Swiss roll and secure with a wooden cocktail stick.

2. Heat the oil in a saucepan with the remaining garlic. When the garlic begins to colour, remove and discard it. Add the pancetta to the pan and cook over a medium heat, stirring frequently, for 2–3 minutes. Reduce the heat to low, add the beef rolls and cook, turning occasionally, for 8–10 minutes until brown all over. Add the tomatoes to the pan, season to taste with salt and pepper, if using, and simmer, stirring occasionally, for 25–30 minutes until the sauce has thickened.

3. Meanwhile, add 1–2 teaspoons of salt, if using, to a large saucepan of water and bring to the boil. Add the pasta, bring back to the boil and cook for 8–10 minutes, or until tender but still firm to the bite. Drain well.

4. Remove the beef rolls from the sauce and add the pasta to the sauce. Toss with two forks, then divide between four plates. Top each portion with a sliced beef roll, sprinkle with the remaining cheese and serve immediately.

LINGUINE WITH
BACON & OLIVES

SERVES: *4* | **PREP:** *15–20 mins* | **COOK:** *15 mins*

INGREDIENTS

3 tbsp olive oil

2 onions, thinly sliced

2 garlic cloves, finely chopped

175 g/6 oz rindless lean bacon,
    diced

225 g/8 oz mushrooms, sliced

5 canned anchovy fillets, drained

6 black olives, stoned and halved

450 g/1 lb dried linguine

25 g/1 oz freshly grated Parmesan
    cheese

salt and pepper (optional)

1. Heat the oil in a large frying pan. Add the onions, garlic and bacon and cook over a low heat, stirring occasionally, until the onions are soft. Stir in the mushrooms, anchovies and olives, then season to taste with salt and pepper, if using. Simmer for 5 minutes.

2. Meanwhile, add 1–2 teaspoons of salt, if using, to a large saucepan of water and bring to the boil. Add the pasta, bring back to the boil and cook for 8–10 minutes, or until tender but still firm to the bite.

3. Drain the pasta and transfer to a warmed serving dish. Spoon the sauce on top, lightly toss together, then sprinkle with the cheese. Serve immediately.

RIGATONI WITH CHORIZO & MUSHROOMS

SERVES: *4* | **PREP:** *15 mins* | **COOK:** *25 mins*

INGREDIENTS

4 tbsp olive oil
1 red onion, chopped
1 garlic clove, chopped
1 celery stick, sliced
400 g/14 oz dried rigatoni
280 g/10 oz chorizo sausage, sliced
225 g/8 oz chestnut mushrooms,
  halved
1 tbsp chopped fresh coriander
1 tbsp lime juice
salt and pepper (optional)

1. Heat the oil in a frying pan. Add the onion, garlic and celery and cook over a low heat, stirring occasionally, for 5 minutes until soft.

2. Meanwhile, add 1–2 teaspoons of salt, if using, to a large saucepan of water and bring to the boil. Add the pasta, bring back to the boil and cook for 8–10 minutes until tender but still firm to the bite.

3. Add the chorizo to the frying pan and cook, stirring occasionally, for 5 minutes until brown all over. Add the mushrooms and cook, stirring occasionally, for a further 5 minutes. Stir in the coriander and lime juice and season to taste with salt and pepper, if using.

4. Drain the pasta and return it to the pan. Add the chorizo and mushroom mixture and toss. Divide between warmed plates and serve immediately.

SKINNY CARBONARA

SERVES: *4* | **PREP:** *20 mins* | **COOK:** *18–20 mins*

INGREDIENTS

300 g/10½ oz dried spaghetti

2 large eggs

*55 g/2 oz freshly grated Parmesan
cheese*

*2 tbsp chopped fresh flat-leaf
parsley*

*115 g/4 oz pancetta or smoked
dry-cure streaky bacon rashers,
chopped*

1 tsp olive oil

70 g/2½ oz reduced-fat soft cheese

salt and pepper (optional)

1. Add 1–2 teaspoons of salt, if using, to a large saucepan of water
and bring to the boil. Add the spaghetti, bring back to the boil and
cook for 8–10 minutes, or until tender but still firm to the bite.

2. Meanwhile whisk together the eggs, half the Parmesan cheese and
the parsley with a fork. Place the pancetta and oil in a large frying
pan and gently heat until the bacon fat starts to run, then fry for 2
minutes, or until lightly browned.

3. Drain the spaghetti, reserving 150 ml/5 fl oz of the hot cooking
water. Add the cooking water and soft cheese to the bacon pan, then
heat, stirring, until melted and smooth. Remove from the heat.

4. Working quickly, add the hot spaghetti to the bacon pan, pour
in the egg mixture and toss – the heat from the pasta and the pan
will thicken the sauce to a coating consistency. Season to taste with
pepper, if using, and divide between warmed bowls. Sprinkle with
the remaining Parmesan cheese and serve immediately.

PEPPERONI PASTA

SERVES: *4* | **PREP:** *10 mins* | **COOK:** *20 mins*

INGREDIENTS

3 tbsp olive oil

1 onion, chopped

1 red pepper, deseeded and diced

1 orange pepper, deseeded and diced

800 g/1 lb 12 oz canned chopped tomatoes

1 tbsp sun-dried tomato purée

1 tsp paprika

225 g/8 oz pepperoni sausage, sliced

2 tbsp chopped fresh flat-leaf parsley, plus extra to garnish

450 g/1 lb dried penne

salt and pepper (optional)

1. Heat 2 tablespoons of the oil in a large, heavy-based frying pan. Add the onion and cook over a low heat, stirring occasionally, for 5 minutes, or until soft. Add the red pepper, orange pepper, tomatoes and their can juices, the sun-dried tomato purée and paprika and bring to the boil.

2. Add the pepperoni and parsley and season to taste with salt and pepper, if using. Stir well, bring to the boil, then reduce the heat and simmer for 10–15 minutes.

3. Meanwhile, add 1–2 teaspoons of salt, if using, to a large saucepan of water and bring to the boil. Add the pasta, bring back to the boil and cook for 8–10 minutes, or until tender but still firm to the bite. Drain well and transfer to a warmed serving dish. Add the remaining oil and toss. Add the sauce and toss again. Sprinkle with parsley and serve immediately.

SPAGHETTI WITH BACON-TOMATO SAUCE

SERVES: *6* | **PREP:** *10 mins* | **COOK:** *40 mins*

INGREDIENTS

55 g/2 oz bacon

1 shallot, diced

2 garlic cloves, finely chopped

4 tbsp red wine

*800 g/1 lb 12 oz canned chopped
    tomatoes*

*425 g/15 oz dried wholewheat
    spaghetti*

*2 tbsp freshly grated Parmesan
    cheese*

salt and pepper (optional)

1. Heat a large frying pan over a medium–high heat. Add the bacon and cook for about 3 minutes on each side, or until crisp. Drain on kitchen paper, then crumble and set aside.

2. Remove the excess bacon fat from the pan, retaining about 2 teaspoons. Add the shallot and garlic and cook, stirring occasionally, over a medium–high heat for about 5 minutes, or until soft. Add the wine, and salt and pepper to taste, if using, and bring to the boil. Add the cooked bacon along with the tomatoes and their can juices and bring to the boil. Reduce the heat to medium and simmer, uncovered, for about 20 minutes.

3. Meanwhile, add 1–2 teaspoons of salt, if using, to a large saucepan of water and bring to the boil. Add the spaghetti, bring back to the boil and cook for 8–10 minutes until tender but still firm to the bite. Drain well.

4. Divide the pasta between six wide pasta bowls, top with the tomato sauce, garnish with the cheese and serve immediately.

TUROS CSUSZA

SERVES: *6* | **PREP:** *10 mins* | **COOK:** *20 mins*

INGREDIENTS

450 g/1 lb dried pasta spirals or
  elbow macaroni
4 smoked back bacon rashers
450 ml/15 fl oz soured cream
350 g/12 oz cottage cheese
salt (optional)

1. Preheat the oven to 180°C/350°F/Gas Mark 4 and preheat the grill. Add 1–2 teaspoons of salt, if using, to a large saucepan of water and bring to the boil, then add the pasta, bring back to the boil and cook for 8–10 minutes until tender but still firm to the bite.

2. Meanwhile, cook the bacon under the preheated grill for 3–4 minutes on each side until crisp. Remove from the heat and crumble into small pieces.

3. Drain the pasta, tip into an ovenproof dish and stir in the soured cream. Sprinkle with the cottage cheese, then with the crumbled bacon and lightly season with salt, if using. Bake in the preheated oven for 5 minutes, then serve straight from the dish.

SAUSAGE, BEAN & ROAST SQUASH CONCHIGLIE

SERVES: *4* | **PREP:** *30 mins* | **COOK:** *45–50 mins*

INGREDIENTS

*1.25 kg/2 lb 12 oz butternut
squash, peeled, deseeded and cut
into 2.5-cm/1-inch chunks*

3 tbsp olive oil

1 onion, finely chopped

1 celery stick, finely chopped

*225 g/8 oz pork sausages with
herbs, skins removed*

100 ml/3½ fl oz red wine

*200 ml /7 fl oz vegetable or chicken
stock*

3 tbsp sun-dried tomato purée

*400 g/14 oz canned borlotti beans,
drained and rinsed*

280 g/10 oz dried conchiglie

*4 tbsp chopped fresh flat-leaf
parsley*

25 g/1 oz pecorino cheese, grated

salt and pepper (optional)

1. Preheat the oven to 200°C/400°F/Gas Mark 6. Place the squash in a roasting tin large enough to fit it in a single layer. Drizzle over 2 tablespoons of the oil. Toss together and roast in the preheated oven for 25–30 minutes until tender.

2. Meanwhile, heat the remaining oil in a large frying pan. Add the onion and celery and fry gently for 2 minutes until the onion is translucent. Increase the heat and add the sausage. Fry for a further 2–3 minutes until lightly browned, breaking the sausage into small pieces as you stir.

3. Add the wine to the pan and boil rapidly until most of it has evaporated. Add the stock, sun-dried tomato purée and beans. Simmer for 10–12 minutes until the liquid is reduced.

4. Add 1–2 teaspoons of salt, if using, to a large saucepan of water and bring to the boil. Add the pasta, bring back to the boil and cook for 8–10 minutes, or until tender but still firm to the bite. Drain and transfer to a warmed serving bowl. Add the squash, sausage sauce and parsley, and season to taste with salt and pepper, if using. Sprinkle over the cheese and serve immediately.

CREAMY BOLOGNESE PASTA

INGREDIENTS

2 tbsp olive oil

1 onion, finely chopped

500 g/1 lb 2 oz fresh pork mince

100 ml/3½ fl oz dry white wine

1 celery stick, chopped

1 garlic clove, crushed

2 bay leaves

200 ml/7 fl oz passata

100 ml/3½ fl oz double cream

450 g/1 lb dried penne

salt (optional)

1. Heat the oil in a large saucepan over a high heat, add the onion and pork and fry, stirring, until lightly browned.

2. Stir in the wine, celery, garlic, bay leaves and passata and bring to the boil. Reduce the heat, cover and simmer for 15 minutes.

3. Remove and discard the bay leaves. Stir in the cream and heat until boiling.

4. Meanwhile, add 1–2 teaspoons of salt, if using, to a large saucepan of water and bring to the boil. Add the pasta, bring back to the boil and cook for 8–10 minutes until tender but still firm to the bite. Drain and combine with the sauce.

5. Transfer to warmed serving bowls and serve immediately.

FARFALLE WITH GORGONZOLA & HAM

SERVES: *4* | **PREP:** *15 mins* | **COOK:** *20 mins*

INGREDIENTS

225 ml/8 fl oz crème fraîche

225 g/8 oz chestnut mushrooms, quartered

400 g/14 oz dried farfalle

85 g/3 oz Gorgonzola cheese, crumbled

1 tbsp chopped fresh flat-leaf parsley

175 g/6 oz cooked ham, diced

salt and pepper (optional)

1. Pour the crème fraîche into a saucepan, add the mushrooms and season to taste with salt and pepper, if using. Bring to just below the boil, then reduce the heat and simmer very gently, stirring occasionally, for 8–10 minutes until the cream has thickened.

2. Meanwhile, add 1–2 teaspoons of salt, if using, to a large saucepan of water and bring to the boil. Add the pasta, bring back to the boil and cook for 8–10 minutes, or until tender but still firm to the bite.

3. Remove the mushrooms from the heat and stir in the cheese until it has melted. Return the pan to a very low heat and stir in the parsley and ham.

4. Drain the pasta and add it to the sauce. Lightly toss, then divide between four serving plates and serve.

SAFFRON LINGUINE

INGREDIENTS

350 g/12 oz dried linguine

pinch of saffron threads

2 tbsp water

140 g/5 oz cooked ham, cut into
strips

175 ml/6 fl oz double cream

55 g/2 oz freshly grated Parmesan
cheese

2 egg yolks

salt and pepper (optional)

1. Add 1–2 teaspoons of salt, if using, to a large saucepan of water and bring to the boil. Add the pasta, bring back to the boil and cook for 8–10 minutes, or until tender but still firm to the bite.

2. Meanwhile, place the saffron in a saucepan with the water. Bring to the boil, remove from the heat and leave to stand for 5 minutes.

3. Stir the ham, cream and cheese into the saffron and return the pan to the heat. Season to taste with salt and pepper, if using, and heat through gently, stirring constantly, until simmering.

4. Remove from the heat and beat in the egg yolks. Drain the pasta and transfer to a warmed serving dish. Add the saffron sauce, toss well to combine and serve immediately.

SPICY PASTA
AMATRICIANA

SERVES: *4* | **PREP:** *20 mins* | **COOK:** *45 mins*

INGREDIENTS

2 tbsp olive oil

1 large onion, finely chopped

2 garlic cloves, finely chopped

175 g/6 oz pancetta or bacon, diced

*1–2 red chillies, deseeded and
   chopped or ½–1 tsp crushed
   dried chillies*

3 tbsp dry white wine

*800 g/1 lb 12 oz canned chopped
   tomatoes*

*450 g/1 lb dried bucatini or
   spaghetti*

85 g/3 oz pecorino cheese, grated

salt and pepper (optional)

1. Heat the oil in a large saucepan, add the onion and garlic and cook over a low heat, stirring occasionally, for 5 minutes. Add the pancetta and chillies, increase the heat to medium and cook, stirring frequently, for 5–8 minutes until the onion is lightly browned.

2. Pour in the wine, bring to the boil and boil rapidly for 2 minutes, then stir in the tomatoes and season to taste with salt and pepper, if using. Bring back to the boil, then reduce the heat to low and simmer, stirring occasionally, for 15 minutes.

3. Meanwhile, add 1–2 teaspoons of salt, if using, to a large saucepan of water and bring to the boil. Add the pasta, bring back to the boil and cook for 8–10 minutes until tender but still firm to the bite.

4. Drain the pasta, tip into the pan with the sauce and toss to coat. Transfer to a warmed serving dish, sprinkle with half the cheese and serve immediately with the remaining cheese on the side.

CHAPTER FOUR

FISH & SEAFOOD

SALAD NIÇOISE

SERVES: *4–6* | **PREP:** *20 mins* | **COOK:** *25 mins*

INGREDIENTS

350 g/12 oz dried conchiglie

2 tuna steaks, about 2 cm/¾ inch thick

olive oil, for brushing

250 g/9 oz French beans, topped and tailed

ready-made garlic vinaigrette, to taste

2 hearts of lettuce, leaves separated

3 large hard-boiled eggs, halved

2 juicy tomatoes, cut into wedges

50 g/1¾ oz anchovy fillets in oil, drained

55 g/2 oz stoned black or Niçoise olives

salt and pepper (optional)

1. Add 1–2 teaspoons of salt, if using, to a large saucepan of water and bring to the boil. Add the pasta, bring back to the boil and cook for 8–10 minutes until tender but still firm to the bite. Drain, refresh in cold water and set aside.

2. Heat a ridged griddle pan over a high heat. Brush the tuna steaks with oil on one side, then place oiled-side down on the hot pan and chargrill for 2 minutes.

3. Lightly brush the top side of the tuna steaks with a little more oil. Turn the steaks over, then season to taste with salt and pepper, if using. Cook for a further 2 minutes for rare or for up to 4 minutes for well done. Remove from the pan and leave to cool.

4. Meanwhile, add 1–2 teaspoons of salt to a large saucepan of water and bring to the boil. Add the beans and bring back to the boil, then cook for 3 minutes. Drain and transfer to a large bowl. Pour over the vinaigrette and stir together.

5. To serve, line a serving dish with lettuce leaves and add the cooled pasta. Lift the beans out of the bowl, leaving the excess dressing behind, and pile them in the centre of the dish. Break the tuna into large flakes and arrange it over the beans.

6. Arrange the eggs, tomatoes, anchovy fillets and olives on top and serve immediately.

PASTA SALAD WITH MELON & PRAWNS

SERVES: 6 | **PREP:** *25 mins, plus chilling* | **COOK:** *20 mins*

INGREDIENTS

225 g/8 oz dried green fusilli

5 tbsp extra virgin olive oil

450 g/1 lb cooked prawns

1 Charentais melon

1 Galia melon

1 tbsp red wine vinegar

1 tsp Dijon mustard

pinch of caster sugar

*1 tbsp chopped fresh flat-leaf
    parsley*

1 tbsp chopped fresh basil

*1 oakleaf or quattro stagioni lettuce,
    shredded*

salt and pepper (optional)

*small handful of fresh basil sprigs,
    to garnish*

1. Add 1–2 teaspoons of salt, if using, to a large saucepan of water and bring to the boil. Add the pasta, bring back to the boil and cook for 8–10 minutes until tender but still firm to the bite. Drain, toss with 1 tablespoon of the oil and leave to cool.

2. Meanwhile, peel and devein the prawns, then place them in a large bowl. Halve both the melons and scoop out the seeds with a spoon. Using a melon baller or teaspoon, scoop out balls of the flesh and add them to the prawns.

3. Whisk together the remaining oil, the vinegar, mustard, sugar, parsley and basil in a small bowl. Season to taste with salt and pepper, if using. Add the cooled pasta to the prawn and melon mixture and lightly toss, then pour in the dressing and toss again. Cover with clingfilm and chill in the refrigerator for 30 minutes.

4. Make a bed of shredded lettuce on a serving plate. Spoon the pasta salad on top, garnish with basil sprigs and serve immediately.

FISH SOUP
WITH MACARONI

SERVES: *6* | **PREP:** *20–25 mins* | **COOK:** *30–35 mins*

INGREDIENTS

2 tbsp olive oil

2 onions, sliced

1 garlic clove, finely chopped

1 litre/1¾ pints fish stock or water

400 g/14 oz canned chopped
   tomatoes

¼ tsp herbes de Provence

¼ tsp saffron threads

115 g/4 oz dried macaroni

18 live mussels, scrubbed and
   debearded

450 g/1 lb monkfish fillet, cut into
   chunks

225 g/8 oz raw prawns, peeled and
   deveined, tails left on

salt and pepper (optional)

1. Heat the oil in a large, heavy-based saucepan. Add the onions and garlic and cook over a low heat, stirring occasionally, for 5 minutes, or until the onions are soft.

2. Add the stock with the tomatoes and their can juices, the herbs, saffron and pasta and season to taste with salt and pepper, if using. Bring to the boil, then cover and simmer for 15 minutes.

3. Discard any mussels with broken shells or any that refuse to close when tapped. Add the mussels, monkfish and prawns to the pan. Re-cover the pan and simmer for a further 5–10 minutes, until the mussels have opened, the prawns have changed colour and the fish is opaque and flakes easily. Discard any mussels that remain closed.

4. Ladle the soup into warmed bowls and serve immediately.

CLAM &
PASTA SOUP

SERVES: 6 | **PREP:** 10 mins | **COOK:** 30–35 mins

INGREDIENTS

3 tbsp olive oil

1 Spanish onion, finely chopped

3 garlic cloves, finely chopped

600 g/1 lb 5 oz canned chopped
    tomatoes

2 tbsp tomato purée

2 tsp sugar

1 tsp dried oregano

1 litre/1¾ pints vegetable stock

500 g/1 lb 2 oz live clams, scrubbed

175 ml/6 fl oz dry white wine

85 g/3 oz dried conchigliette

3 tbsp chopped fresh flat-leaf
    parsley

salt and pepper (optional)

1. Heat the oil in a large saucepan. Add the onion and garlic and cook over a low heat, stirring occasionally, for 5 minutes until soft. Add the tomatoes, tomato purée, sugar, oregano and stock and season to taste with salt and pepper, if using. Mix well and bring to the boil, then reduce the heat, cover and simmer, stirring occasionally, for a further 5 minutes.

2. Discard any clams with broken shells and any that refuse to close when tapped. Put the clams into a saucepan, add the wine, cover and cook over a high heat, shaking the pan occasionally, for 3–5 minutes.

3. Take the clams off the heat and remove from the liquid with a slotted spoon. Reserve the cooking liquid. Discard any clams that remain closed and remove the remainder from the half shells. Strain the reserved cooking liquid into a bowl and set aside.

4. Add the pasta to the soup and simmer, uncovered, for 10 minutes. Add the cooked clams and the reserved cooking liquid. Stir well and heat gently for 4–5 minutes; do not allow the soup to come to the boil. Taste and adjust the seasoning, if using, stir in the parsley and serve immediately.

SCALLOP SOUP
WITH PASTA

INGREDIENTS

500 g/1 lb 2 oz shelled scallops
350 ml/12 fl oz milk
1.5 litres/2½ pints vegetable stock
250 g/9 oz frozen petits pois
175 g/6 oz dried tagliolini
70 g/2½ oz butter
2 spring onions, finely chopped
175 ml/6 fl oz dry white wine
3 slices of prosciutto, cut into thin
 strips
salt and pepper (optional)
1 tbsp chopped fresh flat-leaf
 parsley, to garnish

1. Slice the scallops in half horizontally and season to taste with salt and pepper, if using.

2. Pour the milk and stock into a saucepan, add a pinch of salt, if using, and bring to the boil. Add the petits pois and pasta, bring back to the boil and cook for 8–10 minutes until the pasta is tender but still firm to the bite.

3. Meanwhile, melt the butter in a frying pan. Add the spring onions and cook over a low heat, stirring occasionally, for 3 minutes. Add the scallops and cook for 45 seconds on each side. Pour in the wine, add the prosciutto and cook for 2–3 minutes.

4. Stir the scallop mixture into the soup, taste and adjust the seasoning, if using, and garnish with the parsley. Serve immediately.

FUSILLI WITH MONKFISH & BROCCOLI

SERVES: *4* | **PREP:** *20 mins* | **COOK:** *25 mins*

INGREDIENTS

115 g/4 oz broccoli florets

3 tbsp olive oil

350 g/12 oz monkfish fillet, skinned and cut into bite-sized pieces

2 garlic cloves, crushed

125 ml/4 fl oz dry white wine

225 ml/8 fl oz double cream

400 g/14 oz dried fusilli

85 g/3 oz Gorgonzola cheese, diced

salt and pepper (optional)

1. Separate the broccoli florets into small sprigs. Add 1–2 teaspoons of salt, if using, to a saucepan of water and bring to the boil, then add the broccoli and cook for 2 minutes. Drain and refresh under cold running water.

2. Heat the oil in a large, heavy-based frying pan. Add the monkfish and garlic and season to taste with salt and pepper, if using. Cook, stirring frequently, for 5 minutes, or until the fish is opaque. Pour in the white wine and cream and cook, stirring occasionally, for 5 minutes, or until the fish is cooked through and the sauce has thickened. Stir in the broccoli florets.

3. Meanwhile, add 1–2 teaspoons of salt, if using, to a large saucepan of water and bring to the boil. Add the pasta, bring back to the boil and cook for 8–10 minutes, or until tender but still firm to the bite. Drain the pasta and tip into the pan with the fish, add the cheese and lightly toss. Serve immediately.

SPAGHETTI ALLA PUTTANESCA

SERVES: *4* | **PREP:** *20 mins* | **COOK:** *30 mins*

INGREDIENTS

3 tbsp olive oil

2 garlic cloves, finely chopped

10 anchovy fillets, drained and chopped

140 g/5 oz black olives, stoned and chopped

1 tbsp capers, rinsed

450 g/1 lb plum tomatoes, peeled, deseeded and chopped

400 g/14 oz dried spaghetti

salt and cayenne pepper (optional)

2 tbsp chopped fresh flat-leaf parsley, to garnish

1. Heat the oil in a heavy-based saucepan. Add the garlic and cook over a low heat, stirring frequently, for 2 minutes. Add the anchovies and mash them to a pulp with a fork.

2. Add the olives, capers and tomatoes and season to taste with cayenne pepper, if using. Cover and simmer for 25 minutes.

3. Meanwhile, add 1–2 teaspoons of salt, if using, to a large saucepan of water and bring to the boil. Add the pasta, bring back to the boil and cook for 8–10 minutes until tender but still firm to the bite.

4. Drain the pasta and transfer to a warmed serving dish. Spoon the anchovy sauce over the pasta and toss.

5. Garnish with the chopped parsley and serve immediately.

SPAGHETTINI WITH QUICK TUNA SAUCE

SERVES: 4 | **PREP:** 15–20 mins | **COOK:** 30 mins

INGREDIENTS

3 tbsp olive oil

4 tomatoes, peeled, deseeded and
  roughly chopped

115 g/4 oz mushrooms, sliced

1 tbsp chopped fresh basil

400 g/14 oz canned tuna, drained

100 ml/3½ fl oz fish stock or
  chicken stock

1 garlic clove, finely chopped

2 tsp chopped fresh marjoram

350 g/12 oz dried spaghettini

salt and pepper (optional)

115 g/4 oz freshly grated Parmesan
  cheese, to serve

1. Heat the oil in a large frying pan. Add the tomatoes and cook over a low heat, stirring occasionally, for 15 minutes, or until pulpy. Add the mushrooms and cook, stirring occasionally, for a further 10 minutes. Stir in the basil, tuna, stock, garlic and marjoram and season to taste with salt and pepper, if using. Cook over a low heat for 5 minutes, or until heated through.

2. Meanwhile, add 1–2 teaspoons of salt, if using, to a large saucepan of water and bring to the boil. Add the pasta, bring back to the boil and cook for 8–10 minutes, or until tender but still firm to the bite.

3. Drain the pasta well, transfer to a warmed serving dish and spoon over the tuna mixture. Serve with the grated cheese.

CUCUMBER SPAGHETTI
& PRAWN SALAD

SERVES: *4* | **PREP:** *20 mins, plus soaking* | **COOK:** *No cooking*

INGREDIENTS

1 cucumber

200 g/7 oz courgette, trimmed

140 g/5 oz rice noodle vermicelli

*225 g/8 oz cooked peeled king
   prawns, thawed if frozen*

*350 g/12 oz mango, stoned, peeled
   and diced*

*1 ruby grapefruit, peeled and cut
   into segments, juice squeezed
   from the membrane and
   reserved*

2 tbsp light olive oil or avocado oil

1 tbsp light soy sauce

grated zest and juice of 1 lime

*2.5-cm/1-inch piece fresh ginger,
   peeled and chopped*

25 g/1 oz fresh mint, finely chopped

1. Press the cucumber through a spiralizer to make thin spaghetti-like strands. Place in a sieve or colander set over a bowl and leave to drain for 15 minutes.

2. Meanwhile, spiralize the courgette and set aside without draining.

3. Add the rice noodles to a bowl, cover with boiling water and leave to soak for 2–3 minutes until soft. Drain, rinse with cold water and drain again.

4. Pat the cucumber dry with kitchen paper, then add it to a large salad bowl with the courgette and rice noodles, then scatter the prawns, mango and grapefruit over the top.

5. Put the oil, soy sauce, lime zest and juice, grapefruit juice and ginger into a bowl and lightly fork together. Pour over the salad, sprinkle with the mint and gently toss. Serve immediately.

SPAGHETTI
& COD

INGREDIENTS

300 g/10½ oz dried spaghetti
200 ml/7 fl oz extra virgin olive oil
1 garlic clove, peeled but left whole
450 g/1 lb cherry tomatoes, halved
pinch of crushed dried chillies
  (optional)
600 g/1 lb 5 oz cod fillets, skinned
  and cut into small chunks
salt and pepper (optional)

1. Add 1–2 teaspoons of salt, if using, to a large saucepan of water and bring to the boil. Add the pasta, bring back to the boil and cook for 8–10 minutes, or until tender but still firm to the bite.

2. Meanwhile, put the oil into a large saucepan, add the garlic and cook over a low heat, stirring occasionally, for a few minutes until the garlic starts to brown, then remove and discard. Add the tomatoes to the pan and season to taste with salt, if using. Increase the heat to high and cook, tossing very occasionally, for 6–7 minutes until lightly browned and concentrated without disintegrating.

3. Add the chillies, if using, and the fish and cook, stirring gently, for 1–2 minutes. Add a ladleful of the cooking water from the pasta and taste and adjust the seasoning, if using. Drain the pasta, tip it into the sauce and toss together. Remove from the heat, spoon into warmed bowls and serve immediately.

SEA BASS WITH OLIVE SAUCE

SERVES: *4* | **PREP:** *15–20 mins* | **COOK:** *30–35 mins*

INGREDIENTS

450 g/1 lb dried rigatoni
1 tbsp olive oil
8 x 115-g/4-oz sea bass fillets
shredded leek and shredded carrot,
*   to garnish*
salt and pepper (optional)

SAUCE

25 g/1 oz butter
4 shallots, chopped
2 tbsp capers
175 g/6 oz green olives, stoned and
*   chopped*
4 tbsp balsamic vinegar
300 ml/10 fl oz fish stock
300 ml/10 fl oz double cream
juice of 1 lemon

1. To make the sauce, melt the butter in a frying pan. Add the shallots and cook over a low heat for 4 minutes. Add the capers and olives and cook for a further 3 minutes.

2. Stir in the vinegar and stock, bring to the boil and reduce by half. Add the cream, stirring constantly, and cook until reduced by half. Season to taste with salt and pepper, if using, and stir in the lemon juice. Remove the pan from the heat, set aside and keep warm.

3. Add 1–2 teaspoons of salt, if using, to a large saucepan of water and bring to the boil. Add the pasta and the oil, bring back to the boil and cook for 8–10 minutes, or until tender but still firm to the bite.

4. Meanwhile, lightly grill the sea bass fillets for 3–4 minutes on each side until cooked through but still moist and delicate.

5. Drain the pasta thoroughly and transfer to a large warmed serving dish. Top the pasta with the fish and pour over the olive sauce. Garnish with shredded leek and carrot and serve immediately.

TAGLIATELLE WITH
SMOKED SALMON & ROCKET

SERVES: *4* | **PREP:** *10 mins* | **COOK:** *20 mins*

INGREDIENTS

350 g/12 oz dried tagliatelle

2 tbsp olive oil

1 garlic clove, finely chopped

115 g/4 oz smoked salmon, cut into
thin strips

55 g/2 oz rocket

salt and pepper (optional)

1. Add 1–2 teaspoons of salt, if using, to a large saucepan of water and bring to the boil. Add the pasta, bring back to the boil and cook for 8–10 minutes, until tender but still firm to the bite.

2. Just before the end of the cooking time, heat the oil in a heavy-based frying pan. Add the garlic and cook over a low heat, stirring constantly, for 1 minute. Do not allow the garlic to brown or it will taste bitter.

3. Add the salmon and rocket. Season to taste with pepper, if using, and cook, stirring constantly, for 1 minute. Remove from the heat.

4. Drain the pasta and transfer to a warmed serving dish. Add the smoked salmon and rocket mixture, lightly toss and serve.

SICILIAN
SWORDFISH PASTA

SERVES: *4* | **PREP:** *20 mins* | **COOK:** *30 mins*

INGREDIENTS

1 tbsp olive oil

4 garlic cloves, peeled

1 onion, chopped

8 black olives, stoned and chopped

4 cornichons (small gherkins), chopped

2 tbsp capers in salt, rinsed and chopped

300 g/10½ oz dried spaghetti or linguine

400 g/14 oz canned chopped tomatoes

450 g/1 lb swordfish, cut into small chunks

salt and pepper (optional)

small handful of fresh basil leaves, to garnish

1. Heat the oil in a deep frying pan and add the garlic. When the garlic begins to colour, remove and discard. Add the onion and cook over a low heat, stirring occasionally, for 8–10 minutes until light golden in colour. Stir in the olives, cornichons and capers, season to taste with salt and pepper, if using, and cook, stirring occasionally, for 5 minutes.

2. Meanwhile, add 1–2 teaspoons of salt, if using, to a large saucepan of water and bring to the boil. Add the pasta, bring back to the boil and cook for 8–10 minutes, or until tender but still firm to the bite.

3. Add the tomatoes to the frying pan, increase the heat to medium and bring to the boil, stirring occasionally, then reduce the heat and simmer for 5 minutes. Add the swordfish chunks, cover and simmer gently for a further 5 minutes.

4. Drain the pasta and tip into a warmed serving dish. Top with the swordfish sauce and tear the basil leaves over it. Serve immediately.

PRAWN & CHILLI-LIME SPAGHETTI

SERVES: *4* | **PREP:** *20 mins* | **COOK:** *30 mins*

INGREDIENTS

450 g/1 lb dried spaghetti

4 garlic cloves

2–4 red or green jalapeño chillies

4 small courgettes

3 spring onions

2 tbsp olive oil

*450 g/1 lb peeled and deveined raw
    prawns*

juice and finely grated zest of 1 lime

2 tbsp butter

salt (optional)

1. Add 1–2 teaspoons of salt, if using, to a large saucepan of water and bring to the boil. Add the spaghetti, bring back to the boil and cook for 8–10 minutes, or until tender but still firm to the bite. Meanwhile, peel and press the garlic, deseed and dice the chillies, dice the courgettes and thinly slice the spring onions.

2. Drain the pasta in a colander and set aside until needed. Return the pan to the heat, add the oil and heat over a medium–high heat. Add the garlic and cook, stirring, for 1–2 minutes, until it begins to soften. Add the chillies, courgettes and salt, if using, and cook, stirring occasionally, until the courgettes are beginning to brown.

3. Add the prawns and lime juice and zest to the pan. Add the spring onions and cook, stirring occasionally, until the prawns are pink and cooked through. Add the butter and the reserved spaghetti and cook, stirring, for 1–2 minutes until most of the liquid has evaporated. Serve immediately.

LEMON PRAWNS
WITH PASTA

SERVES: *4* | **PREP:** *15–20 mins* | **COOK:** *15–20 mins*

INGREDIENTS

125 g/4½ oz butter
125 ml/4 fl oz olive oil
2 shallots, finely chopped
6 garlic cloves, finely chopped
finely grated rind of 1 large lemon
90 ml/3 fl oz dry white wine
2 tbsp lemon juice
600 g/1 lb 5 oz jumbo prawns,
*   peeled and deveined*
2 tbsp finely chopped fresh flat-leaf
*   parsley*
350 g/12 oz dried angel hair pasta
salt and pepper (optional)

1. Melt the butter with the oil in a large frying pan over a medium-high heat. Add the shallots and garlic and fry for 1–2 minutes, until the shallots are soft but not brown.

2. Stir in the lemon rind, wine and lemon juice, bring to the boil and cook, stirring occasionally, for 2–3 minutes until the sauce reduces slightly and the flavours blend. If the butter starts to brown, immediately remove the pan from the heat.

3. Reduce the heat, add the prawns and cook, stirring occasionally, for 2–3 minutes until they turn pink and curl. Stir in the parsley and season to taste with salt and pepper, if using.

4. Meanwhile, add 1–2 teaspoons of salt to a large saucepan of water and bring to the boil. Add the pasta, bring back to the boil and cook for 2–4 minutes, or according to the packet instructions. Drain the pasta well, then immediately add it to the pan with the prawns, using two forks to mix and blend all the ingredients together.

5. Divide the pasta and prawns between warmed bowls, pour the cooking juices over and serve immediately.

CLAMS WITH SPAGHETTI

SERVES: *4* | **PREP:** *10–15 mins* | **COOK:** *10–15 mins*

INGREDIENTS

1 kg/2 lb 4 oz small live clams,
*   scrubbed*
350 g/12 oz dried spaghetti
125 ml/4 fl oz olive oil
4 garlic cloves, chopped
125 ml/4 fl oz dry white wine
4 tbsp chopped fresh flat-leaf
*   parsley*
salt and pepper (optional)

1. Discard any clams with broken shells and any that refuse to close when tapped, then set the remainder aside.

2. Add 1–2 teaspoons of salt, if using, to a large saucepan of water and bring to the boil. Add the spaghetti, bring back to the boil and cook for 2 minutes less than specified in the packet instructions. Remove from the heat and set aside without draining.

3. Meanwhile, heat the oil in a large, deep frying pan over a medium heat. Add the garlic and stir for 1 minute until golden but not brown.

4. Increase the heat to high, add the wine, then bubble for 2 minutes, or until reduced by half. Add the clams and stir for 2–3 minutes until they open. Discard any clams that remain closed.

5. Add 250 ml/9 fl oz of the pasta cooking water to the clam pan. Use a pasta ladle to add the pasta to the pan, and cook, stirring, for a further 2 minutes, or until the pasta is tender but still firm to the bite.

6. Season to taste with salt and pepper, if using. Stir in the parsley and serve immediately.

SPAGHETTI WITH CRAB

INGREDIENTS

*1 dressed crab, about 450 g/1 lb,
    including the shell*
350 g/12 oz dried spaghetti
6 tbsp extra virgin olive oil
*1 fresh red chilli, deseeded and
    finely chopped*
2 garlic cloves, finely chopped
*3 tbsp chopped fresh flat-leaf
    parsley*
2 tbsp lemon juice
1 tsp finely grated lemon rind
salt and pepper (optional)
lemon wedges, to garnish

1. Using a sharp knife, scoop the meat from the crab shell into a bowl. Lightly mix the white and brown meat together and set aside.

2. Add 1–2 teaspoons of salt, if using, to a large saucepan of water and bring to the boil. Add the pasta, bring back to the boil and cook for 8–10 minutes, or until tender but still firm to the bite. Drain thoroughly and return to the pan.

3. Meanwhile, heat 2 tablespoons of the oil in a frying pan over a low heat. Add the chilli and garlic and cook for 30 seconds, then add the crabmeat, parsley, lemon juice and lemon rind. Cook for 1 minute until the crab is just heated through.

4. Add the crab mixture to the pasta with the remaining oil and season to taste with salt and pepper, if using. Toss together thoroughly, transfer to a large, warmed serving dish, garnish with a few lemon wedges and serve immediately.

FETTUCCINE WITH LEMON PEPPER SEAFOOD

SERVES: *4* | **PREP:** *15 mins* | **COOK:** *20 mins*

INGREDIENTS

*5 tbsp lemon pepper oil, plus extra
   to serve*
6 garlic cloves, crushed
*675 g/1 lb 8 oz mixed seafood
   (prawns, squid, mussels)*
dash of vodka
125 ml/4 fl oz white wine
1 fresh tarragon sprig, leaves only
450 g/1 lb fettuccine
*chopped fresh flat-leaf parsley,
   to garnish*
salt and pepper (optional)

1. Heat a wok or deep frying pan and add the oil. When the oil is hot, add the garlic and seafood and stir for 1 minute. Add the vodka, wine, tarragon and a pinch of salt, if using. Stir until the seafood is cooked through.

2. Add 1–2 teaspoons of salt, if using, to a large saucepan of water and bring to the boil. Add the pasta, bring back to the boil and cook for 8–10 minutes, or until tender but still firm to the bite. Drain and add the pasta to the seafood mixture. Toss well and transfer to warmed plates. Drizzle over some oil, garnish with parsley and serve.

FARFALLINI BUTTERED LOBSTER

SERVES: *4* | PREP: *30–35 mins* | COOK: *20–25 mins*

INGREDIENTS

2 lobsters, split into halves, each weighing about 700 g/1 lb 9 oz
juice and grated rind of 1 lemon
115 g/4 oz butter
4 tbsp fresh white breadcrumbs
2 tbsp brandy
5 tbsp double cream or crème fraîche
450 g/1 lb dried farfallini
55 g/2 oz freshly grated Parmesan cheese
salt and pepper (optional)
4 lemon wedges, to garnish
small handful of fresh dill sprigs, to garnish

1. Preheat the oven to 160°C/325°F/Gas Mark 3. Discard the stomach sac, vein and gills from each lobster. Remove the meat from the tail and chop. Crack the claws and legs, remove the meat and chop. Transfer the meat to a bowl and add the lemon juice and rind. Clean the shells and place in the preheated oven to dry out.

2. Melt 25 g/1 oz of the butter in a frying pan. Add the breadcrumbs and cook for 3 minutes until crisp and golden brown. Melt the remaining butter in a saucepan. Add the lobster meat and heat through gently. Add the brandy and cook for a further 3 minutes, then add the cream and season to taste with salt and pepper, if using.

3. Meanwhile, add 1–2 teaspoons of salt, if using, to a large saucepan of water and bring to the boil. Add the pasta, bring back to the boil and cook for 8–10 minutes, or until tender but still firm to the bite. Drain the pasta and spoon into the clean lobster shells.

4. Preheat the grill to medium. Spoon the buttered lobster on top of the pasta and sprinkle with a little cheese and the breadcrumbs. Grill for 2–3 minutes, or until golden brown. Transfer the lobster shells to a warmed plate, garnish with the lemon wedges and dill and serve.

FETTUCCINE & PRAWN PARCELS

SERVES: *4* | **PREP:** *10 mins* | **COOK:** *20–25 mins*

INGREDIENTS

450 g/1 lb dried fettuccine

150 ml/5 fl oz pesto

4 tsp extra virgin olive oil

750 g/1 lb 10 oz large raw prawns, peeled and deveined

2 garlic cloves, crushed

125 ml/4 fl oz dry white wine

salt and pepper (optional)

1. Preheat the oven to 200°C/400°F/Gas Mark 6. Cut out four 30-cm/12-inch squares of greaseproof paper. Add 1–2 teaspoons of salt, if using, to a large saucepan of water and bring to the boil. Add the pasta, bring back to the boil and cook for 2–3 minutes, or until just soft. Drain and set aside.

2. Mix the fettuccine and half of the pesto together in a bowl. Spread out the paper squares and place 1 teaspoon of oil in the centre of each. Divide the fettuccine between the squares, then divide the prawns and place on top of the fettuccine.

3. Mix the remaining pesto and the garlic together and spoon over the prawns. Season each parcel to taste with salt and pepper, if using, and sprinkle with the wine. Dampen the edges of the paper and loosely wrap the parcels, twisting the edges to seal.

4. Place the parcels on a baking sheet and bake in the preheated oven for 10–15 minutes. Transfer the parcels to warmed plates and serve immediately.

SPRINGTIME PASTA

SERVES: *4* | **PREP:** *25 mins* | **COOK:** *25–30 mins*

INGREDIENTS

2 tbsp lemon juice

4 baby globe artichokes

7 tbsp olive oil

2 shallots, finely chopped

2 garlic cloves, finely chopped

2 tbsp chopped fresh flat-leaf
*   parsley*

2 tbsp chopped fresh mint

350 g/12 oz dried rigatoni

25 g/1 oz unsalted butter

2 large raw prawns, peeled and
*   deveined*

salt and pepper (optional)

1. Fill a bowl with cold water and add the lemon juice. Prepare the artichokes one at a time. Cut off the stems and trim away any tough outer leaves. Cut across the tops of the leaves. Slice in half lengthways and remove the central fibrous chokes, then cut lengthways into 5-mm/¼-inch thick slices. Immediately place the slices in the bowl of acidulated water to prevent discoloration.

2. Heat 5 tablespoons of the oil in a heavy-based frying pan. Drain the artichoke slices and pat dry with kitchen paper. Add them to the pan with the shallots, garlic, parsley and mint and cook over a low heat, stirring frequently, for 10–12 minutes until tender.

3. Meanwhile, add 1–2 teaspoons of salt, if using, to a large saucepan of water and bring to the boil. Add the pasta, bring back to the boil and cook for 8–10 minutes, or until tender but still firm to the bite.

4. Melt the butter in a small frying pan and add the prawns. Cook, stirring occasionally, for 2–3 minutes until opaque and firm to the touch. Season to taste with salt and pepper, if using.

5. Drain the pasta and tip it into a bowl. Add the remaining oil and toss. Add the artichoke mixture and the prawns and toss again. Spoon into warmed bowls and serve immediately.

CHAPTER FIVE

FILLED
& BAKED

WARM RAVIOLI SALAD

SERVES: *4* | **PREP:** *20 mins* | **COOK:** *15 mins*

INGREDIENTS

125 ml/4 fl oz olive oil

2 tbsp balsamic vinegar

1 tsp Dijon mustard

1 tsp sugar

½ small cucumber, peeled

225 g/8 oz mixed lettuce leaves

115 g/4 oz rocket

1 head of chicory, sliced

3 tbsp mixed chopped herbs, such
*   as parsley, thyme and coriander*

2 tomatoes, cut into wedges

2 red peppers or yellow peppers in
*   oil, drained and sliced*

20 fresh beef ravioli

25 g/1 oz butter

salt and pepper (optional)

1. Whisk 100 ml/3½ fl oz of the oil, the vinegar, mustard and sugar together in a bowl and season to taste with salt and pepper, if using. Set aside.

2. Halve the cucumber lengthways and scoop out the seeds, then slice. Tear the lettuce and rocket leaves into small pieces. Put the cucumber, lettuce, rocket, chicory, herbs, tomatoes and red peppers into a bowl and set aside.

3. Add 1–2 teaspoons of salt, if using, to a large saucepan of water and bring to the boil. Add the ravioli and cook according to the packet instructions, then drain. Melt the butter with the remaining oil in a frying pan. Add the ravioli and cook over a medium heat, turning carefully once or twice, for 5 minutes until golden on both sides. Remove the pan from the heat.

4. Pour the dressing over the salad and toss, then divide between individual serving plates. Top with the ravioli and serve immediately.

PASTA IN CHICKEN SOUP

SERVES: *4* | **PREP:** *15–20 mins* | **COOK:** *1 hour 30 mins – 1 hour 35 mins*

INGREDIENTS

*1 x 1.6-kg/3 lb 8-oz oven-ready
    chicken, cut into pieces and
    skinned*
2 bay leaves
1 large carrot, roughly chopped
*1 large celery stick with leaves,
    roughly chopped*
*1 large onion, unpeeled, cut into
    quarters*
2 litres/3½ pints water
*5-cm/2-inch piece Parmesan cheese
    rind*
300 g/10½ oz fresh tortelloni
salt and pepper (optional)
*4 tbsp freshly grated Parmesan
    cheese, to serve*

1. Put the chicken, bay leaves, carrot, celery, onion and 2 teaspoons of salt, if using, into a large stockpot or deep saucepan. Pour in the water and slowly bring to just below boiling point, skimming the surface occasionally to remove the scum. Do not allow to boil.

2. Reduce the heat to low, cover and simmer for 1 hour. Skim the surface again, if necessary. Stir in the cheese rind, re-cover and simmer for a further 20 minutes, or until the chicken is tender and the juices run clear when a skewer is inserted into the thickest part of the meat. Remove the chicken pieces (and set aside if using for the main course). Remove and discard the cheese rind.

3. Strain the liquid into a large bowl, pressing down on the vegetables. Skim the surface, then transfer 1.2 litres/2 pints of the broth to a large saucepan. Add salt and pepper to taste, if using.

4. Bring to the boil, add the tortelloni and cook for 2 minutes, or according to the packet instructions, until tender but still firm to the bite.

5. Ladle the pasta and broth into bowls and serve with the grated cheese for sprinkling.

SPINACH & TOMATO
TORTELLINI SOUP

SERVES: *4* | **PREP:** *15 mins* | **COOK:** *30 mins*

INGREDIENTS

4 tbsp olive oil

1 onion, thinly sliced

2 garlic cloves, finely chopped

900 ml/1½ pints chicken stock

*500 g/1 lb 2 oz fresh or frozen
chicken or pork tortellini*

*400 g/14 oz canned chopped
tomatoes*

1 tbsp sun-dried tomato purée

*400 g/14 oz canned borlotti beans,
drained and rinsed*

*350 g/12 oz spinach, rinsed and
drained, coarse stalks removed*

*2 tbsp chopped fresh flat-leaf
parsley*

salt and pepper (optional)

*25 g/1 oz freshly grated Parmesan
cheese, to serve*

1. Heat the oil in a saucepan, add the onion and garlic and cook over a low heat, stirring occasionally, for 5 minutes until soft. Add the stock, increase the heat to medium and bring to the boil.

2. Add the tortellini and cook for 5 minutes, then reduce the heat, Add the tomatoes and their can juices, the tomato purée and beans and season to taste with salt and pepper, if using. Reduce the heat and simmer for a further 5 minutes.

3. Stir in the spinach and parsley and cook for 1–2 minutes until the spinach is just wilted. Remove from the heat and serve immediately, handing the cheese separately.

VEGETABLE
CANNELLONI

SERVES: *4* | **PREP:** *15 mins* | **COOK:** *35–40 mins*

INGREDIENTS

12 dried cannelloni tubes

140 ml /4½ fl oz olive oil, plus extra
  for oiling

1 aubergine, diced

225 g/8 oz spinach

4 garlic cloves, crushed

1 tsp ground cumin

85 g /3 oz mushrooms, chopped

1 onion, finely chopped

800 g/1 lb 12 oz canned chopped
  tomatoes

1 tsp caster sugar

2 tbsp fresh basil

55 g/2 oz mozzarella cheese, sliced

salt and pepper (optional

lamb's lettuce, to garnish

1. Preheat the oven to 190°C/375°F/Gas Mark 5. Lightly oil a large ovenproof dish.

2. Add 1–2 teaspoons of salt, if using, to a large saucepan of water and bring to the boil. Add the cannelloni tubes, bring back to the boil and cook for 8–10 minutes, or until tender but still firm to the bite. Drain on kitchen paper and pat dry.

3. Heat 125 ml/4 fl oz of the oil in a frying pan over a medium heat. Add the aubergine and cook, stirring frequently, for 2–3 minutes.

4. Add the spinach, half the garlic, the cumin and mushrooms and reduce the heat. Season to taste with salt and pepper, if using, and cook, stirring, for about 2–3 minutes. Spoon the mixture into the cannelloni tubes and put into the prepared dish in a single layer.

5. Heat the remaining oil in a saucepan over a medium heat. Add the onion and the remaining garlic and cook for 1 minute. Add the tomatoes, sugar and basil and bring to the boil. Reduce the heat and simmer for 5 minutes. Spoon the sauce over the cannelloni tubes.

6. Arrange the cheese over the top of the cannelloni tubes and bake in the preheated oven for about 30 minutes, or until the cheese is golden brown and bubbling. Serve immediately, garnished with lamb's lettuce.

PUMPKIN RAVIOLI

SERVES: *4* | **PREP:** *30 mins, plus chilling and resting* | **COOK:** *30–35 mins*

INGREDIENTS

300 g/10½ oz durum wheat flour,
plus extra for dusting

2 eggs

1 tbsp olive oil

1 tsp vinegar

3–4 tbsp water

salt (optional)

FILLING

1 tbsp olive oil

450 g/1 lb pumpkin, cubed

1 shallot, finely diced

125 ml/4 fl oz water

55 g/2 oz freshly grated Parmesan
cheese

1 egg

1 tbsp finely chopped fresh parsley

salt and pepper (optional)

1. Put the flour, eggs, oil, ½ teaspoon of salt, if using, the vinegar and water into a bowl and knead to a silky-smooth dough. Wrap the dough in clingfilm and chill in the refrigerator for 1 hour.

2. Meanwhile, to make the filling, heat the oil in a saucepan, add the pumpkin and shallot and sauté for 2–3 minutes, or until the shallot is translucent. Add the water and cook for 15–20 minutes, or until the liquid evaporates. Leave to cool slightly, then mix with the cheese, egg and parsley. Season to taste with salt and pepper, if using.

3. Divide the dough in half and thinly roll out both pieces. Place small spoonfuls of the pumpkin mixture, spaced about 4 cm/1½ inches apart, on one sheet of dough. Brush a little water on the spaces in between. Lay the second sheet of dough on top and press down around each piece of filling.

4. Use a pastry wheel to cut out squares and press the edges together with a fork. Leave the ravioli to dry for 30 minutes, then add 1–2 teaspoons of salt, if using, to a large saucepan of water and bring to the boil. Add the ravioli, bring back to the boil and cook over a medium heat for 8–10 minutes, until tender but still firm to the bite. Remove the ravioli with a slotted spoon and drain well on kitchen paper. Serve immediately.

BROCCOLI & MASCARPONE CANNELLONI

SERVES: *4* | **PREP:** *25–30 mins* | **COOK:** *1 hour 25 mins*

INGREDIENTS

12 dried cannelloni tubes

6 tbsp olive oil, plus extra for
*   brushing*

4 shallots, finely chopped

1 garlic clove, finely chopped

600 g/1 lb 5 oz plum tomatoes,
*   peeled, deseeded and chopped*

3 red peppers, deseeded and
*   chopped*

1 tbsp sun-dried tomato purée

1 tbsp shredded fresh basil leaves

450 g/1 lb broccoli, broken into
*   florets*

85 g/3 oz fresh breadcrumbs

150 ml/5 fl oz milk

225 g/8 oz mascarpone cheese

pinch of freshly grated nutmeg

6 tbsp grated pecorino cheese

2 tbsp flaked almonds

salt and pepper (optional)

1. Preheat the oven to 190°C/375°F/Gas Mark 5. Add 1–2 teaspoons of salt, if using, to a large saucepan of water and bring to the boil. Add the pasta, bring back to the boil and cook for 8–10 minutes, or until tender but still firm to the bite. Transfer the pasta to a plate and pat dry with kitchen paper. Brush a large ovenproof dish with oil.

2. Heat 2 tablespoons of the oil in a frying pan. Add the shallots and garlic and cook over a low heat for 5 minutes, or until soft. Add the tomatoes, red peppers and sun-dried tomato purée and season to taste with salt and pepper, if using. Bring to the boil, then reduce the heat and simmer for 20 minutes. Stir in the basil and pour the sauce into the dish.

3. Meanwhile, add 1–2 teaspoons of salt, if using, to a saucepan of water and bring to the boil. Add the broccoli and cook for 10 minutes, or until tender. Drain, then process to a purée in a food processor or blender.

4. Mix the breadcrumbs, milk and remaining oil together in a large bowl, then stir in the mascarpone cheese, nutmeg, broccoli purée and 4 tablespoons of the pecorino cheese. Season to taste with salt and pepper, if using.

5. Fill the cannelloni tubes with the broccoli mixture and place them in the prepared dish. Brush with oil and sprinkle with the remaining pecorino cheese and the almonds. Bake in the preheated oven for 25 minutes until golden and bubbling. Serve immediately.

ZITI AL FORNO

SERVES: *4* | **PREP:** *15–20 mins* | **COOK:** *35–50 mins, plus standing*

INGREDIENTS

olive oil, for oiling
350 g/12 oz dried ziti or penne
250 g/9 oz ricotta cheese
250 g/9 oz mozzarella cheese,
*   grated*
85 g/3 oz freshly grated Parmesan
*   cheese*
750 ml/1¼ pints ready-made
*   tomato sauce with herbs*
2 tbsp chopped fresh parsley
salt and pepper (optional)

1. Preheat the oven to 220°C/425°F/Gas Mark 7 and lightly oil a large baking dish.

2. Add 1–2 teaspoons of salt, if using, to a large saucepan of water and bring to the boil. Add the ziti, bring back to the boil and cook for 2 minutes less than specified in the packet instructions.

3. Meanwhile, beat together the ricotta cheese, half the mozzarella cheese and a third of the Parmesan cheese in a large bowl. Season to taste with salt and pepper, if using, and set aside.

4. Just before the pasta finishes cooking, take 4 tablespoons of the pasta cooking liquid and beat it into the cheese mixture until a creamy sauce starts to form.

5. Drain the pasta, add it to the cheese bowl and stir until coated with cheese. Add the tomato sauce and parsley and stir until well mixed.

6. Tip the pasta into the prepared baking dish and smooth the surface. Sprinkle over the remaining mozzarella cheese and Parmesan cheese.

7. Place the dish on a baking sheet and bake in the preheated oven for 25–30 minutes until golden brown on top. Leave to stand for a few minutes, then serve straight from the dish.

FOUR-CHEESE
MACARONI

SERVES: *4* | **PREP:** *15–20 mins* | **COOK:** *30–40 mins, plus standing*

INGREDIENTS

*85 g/3 oz freshly grated Parmesan
  cheese*

55 g/2 oz fine dry breadcrumbs

400 g/14 oz dried macaroni

*40 g/1½ oz butter, plus extra for
  greasing*

40 g/1½ oz plain flour

600 ml/1 pint lukewarm milk

*pinch of freshly grated nutmeg, or
  to taste*

*85 g/3 oz dolcelatte cheese, finely
  chopped*

*85 g/3 oz provolone or Taleggio
  cheese, grated*

55 g/2 oz mozzarella cheese, diced

olive oil, for drizzling

salt and pepper (optional)

1. Preheat the oven to 200°C/400°F/Gas Mark 6. Lightly grease a large baking dish with butter, then set aside. Mix a third of the Parmesan cheese with the breadcrumbs and set aside.

2. Add 1–2 teaspoons of salt, if using, to a large saucepan of water and bring to the boil. Add the macaroni, bring back to the boil and cook for 2 minutes less than specified in the packet instructions. Drain well, rinse with cold water, drain again and set aside.

3. Meanwhile, melt the butter in a saucepan over a medium heat. Sprinkle over the flour and stir for 2 minutes until blended. Remove the pan from the heat and gradually add the milk, stirring constantly to prevent lumps forming.

4. Return the pan to the heat, stir in the nutmeg and season to taste with salt and pepper, if using. Slowly bring to the boil, stirring, until the sauce thickens. Stir in the remaining Parmesan cheese, the dolcelatte cheese and the provolone cheese and continue stirring until the cheese melts and is blended. Stir in the mozzarella cheese.

5. Add the macaroni and stir to coat in the sauce. Adjust the seasoning, if using. Tip the mixture into the prepared dish and smooth the surface. Sprinkle the breadcrumb mixture over the top and drizzle with oil.

6. Place the dish on a baking sheet and bake in the preheated oven for 20–25 minutes, until golden brown on top. Leave to stand for a few minutes, then serve straight from the dish.

CANNELLONI WITH CHICKEN & HAM

SERVES: *4* | **PREP:** *20 mins* | **COOK:** *1¼–1½ hours*

INGREDIENTS

1 tbsp olive oil, plus extra for
brushing
1 small onion, finely chopped
175 g/6 oz fresh chicken mince
115 g/4 oz cooked ham, finely
chopped
70 g/2½ oz cream cheese with
garlic and herbs
8 dried no pre-cook cannelloni tubes
4 tbsp freshly grated Parmesan
cheese
salt and pepper (optional)

TOMATO SAUCE

25 g/1 oz butter
2 tbsp olive oil
1 onion, finely chopped
2 garlic cloves, finely chopped
1 celery stick, finely chopped
400 g/14 oz canned chopped
tomatoes
2 tbsp tomato purée
brown sugar, to taste
1 tbsp chopped fresh flat-leaf
parsley
100 ml/3½ fl oz water
salt and pepper (optional)

1. First, make the sauce. Melt the butter with the oil in a saucepan. Add the onion, garlic and celery and cook over a low heat, stirring occasionally, for 5 minutes until soft. Stir in the tomatoes, tomato purée, sugar to taste, parsley and water and season to taste with salt and pepper, if using. Increase the heat to medium and bring to the boil, then reduce the heat and simmer, stirring occasionally, for 20–30 minutes until thickened.

2. Meanwhile, preheat the oven to 190°C/375°F/Gas Mark 5. Brush an ovenproof dish with oil. Heat the oil in a frying pan, add the onion and cook over a low heat, stirring occasionally, for 5 minutes until soft. Add the chicken and cook, stirring frequently, for a further few minutes until lightly browned. Remove the pan from the heat, stir in the ham and cream cheese and season to taste with salt and pepper, if using.

3. Fill the cannelloni tubes with the chicken mixture and put them into the prepared dish. Pour the sauce over them, sprinkle with the Parmesan cheese and bake in the preheated oven for 35–40 minutes until cooked through. Serve immediately.

BAKED PASTA
WITH MUSHROOMS

SERVES: *4* | **PREP:** *10–15 mins* | **COOK:** *25–30 mins*

INGREDIENTS

140 g/5 oz fontina cheese, thinly
sliced
600 ml/1 pint béchamel sauce
6 tbsp butter, plus extra for greasing
350 g/12 oz mixed wild mushrooms,
sliced
350 g/12 oz dried tagliatelle
2 egg yolks
4 tbsp grated romano cheese
salt and pepper (optional)
mixed salad leaves, to serve

1. Preheat the oven to 200°C/400°F/Gas Mark 6. Stir the fontina cheese into the béchamel sauce and set aside.

2. Put 2 tablespoons of the butter into a large saucepan and heat over a low heat until melted. Add the mushrooms and cook, stirring occasionally, for 10 minutes.

3. Meanwhile, add 1–2 teaspoons of salt, if using, to a large saucepan of water and bring to the boil. Add the pasta, bring back to the boil and cook for 8–10 minutes, or until tender but still firm to the bite. Drain, return to the pan and add the remaining butter, the egg yolks and about a third of the sauce, then season to taste with salt and pepper, if using. Toss well to mix, then gently stir in the mushrooms.

4. Lightly grease a large, ovenproof dish with butter and spoon in the pasta mixture. Pour over the remaining sauce and sprinkle with the romano cheese. Bake in the preheated oven for 15–20 minutes, or until golden brown. Serve immediately with salad leaves.

TURKEY & MUSHROOM CANNELLONI

SERVES: *4* | **PREP:** *25 mins* | **COOK:** *1 hour 35 mins*

INGREDIENTS

butter, for greasing

2 tbsp olive oil

2 garlic cloves, crushed

1 large onion, finely chopped

225 g/8 oz wild mushrooms, sliced

350 g/12 oz fresh turkey mince

115 g/4 oz prosciutto, diced

150 ml/5 fl oz Marsala

200 g/7 oz canned chopped
*   tomatoes*

1 tbsp shredded fresh basil leaves

2 tbsp tomato purée

10–12 dried cannelloni tubes

600 ml/1 pint béchamel sauce

85 g/3 oz freshly grated Parmesan
*   cheese*

salt and pepper (optional)

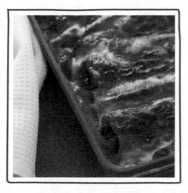

1. Preheat the oven to 190°C/375°F/Gas Mark 5. Lightly grease a large ovenproof dish. Heat the oil in a heavy-based frying pan. Add the garlic, onion and mushrooms and cook over a low heat, stirring frequently, for 8–10 minutes. Add the turkey and prosciutto and cook, stirring frequently, for 12 minutes, or until brown all over. Stir in the Marsala, tomatoes and their can juices, basil and tomato purée and cook for 4 minutes. Season to taste with salt and pepper, if using, then cover and simmer for 30 minutes. Uncover, stir and simmer for 15 minutes.

2. Meanwhile, add 1–2 teaspoons of salt, if using, to a large saucepan of water and bring to the boil. Add the cannelloni tubes, bring back to the boil and cook for 8–10 minutes, or until tender but still firm to the bite. Using a slotted spoon, transfer the cannelloni tubes to a plate and pat dry with kitchen paper.

3. Use a teaspoon to fill the cannelloni tubes with the turkey and mushroom mixture. Transfer them to the dish. Pour the béchamel sauce over them to cover completely and sprinkle with the cheese.

4. Bake in the preheated oven for 30 minutes, or until golden and bubbling. Serve immediately.

CHICKEN & ORZO BAKE

SERVES: *4* | **PREP:** *15 mins* | **COOK:** *40 mins*

INGREDIENTS

100 g/3½ oz ricotta cheese, drained
125 g/4½ oz mozzarella cheese, grated
55 g/2 oz Gruyère cheese, finely grated
125 g/4½ oz dried orzo pasta
2 tbsp olive oil, plus extra for oiling and drizzling
1 large onion, finely chopped
450 g/1 lb fresh chicken mince
4 large garlic cloves, finely chopped
1 tbsp dried mixed herbs
500 ml/18 fl oz passata
40 g/1½ oz fine dried breadcrumbs
salt and pepper (optional)

1. Preheat the oven to 220°C/425°F/Gas Mark 7 and oil a 1.2-litre/2-pint ovenproof serving dish. Beat together the ricotta cheese, mozzarella cheese and half the Gruyère cheese in a large bowl and set aside.

2. Add 1 teaspoon of salt, if using, to a saucepan of water and bring to the boil. Add the pasta, bring back to the boil and cook for 2 minutes less than specified in the packet instructions.

3. Meanwhile, heat the oil in a frying pan over a medium–high heat. Add the onion and fry, stirring, for 2–3 minutes until soft. Add the chicken, garlic and herbs, stirring with a wooden spoon to break up the chicken into large clumps, for about 2 minutes until it loses its raw appearance. Stir in the passata, season to taste with salt and pepper, if using, bring to the boil, then simmer for 10 minutes.

4. Drain the pasta and immediately tip it into the bowl with the cheese. Add the chicken mixture, stirring until the cheeses melt.

5. Pour into the prepared dish and smooth the surface. Combine the remaining Gruyère cheese with the breadcrumbs and sprinkle over the pasta and chicken mixture, then drizzle with oil. Bake in the preheated oven for 20–25 minutes until the top is golden brown and bubbling. Serve immediately.

TURKEY, LEEK & CHEESE CASSEROLE

SERVES: *4* | **PREP:** *20–25 mins* | **COOK:** *40–45 mins*

INGREDIENTS

*115 g/4 oz dried short
   macaroni*
1 small egg, lightly beaten
2 tbsp butter
*4 small leeks, green parts included,
   finely sliced*
2 carrots, diced
1 tbsp plain flour
¼ tsp freshly grated nutmeg
250 ml/9 fl oz chicken stock
*225 g/8 oz diced cooked turkey or
   chicken*
55 g/2 oz diced cooked ham
*3 tbsp chopped fresh flat-leaf
   parsley*
100 g/3½ oz Gruyère cheese, grated
salt and pepper (optional)

1. Preheat the oven to 180°C/350°F/Gas Mark 4. Add 1–2 teaspoons of salt, if using, to a saucepan of water and bring to the boil over a medium heat. Add the pasta, bring back to the boil and cook for 8–10 minutes, or until tender but still firm to the bite. Drain and return to the pan. Stir in the egg and a knob of the butter, mixing well to combine. Set aside.

2. Melt the remaining butter in a saucepan over a medium heat. Add the leeks and carrots. Cover and cook for 5 minutes, shaking the pan occasionally, until just tender.

3. Add the flour and nutmeg and cook for 1 minute, stirring constantly. Pour in the stock and bring to the boil, stirring constantly. Stir in the turkey, ham and parsley. Season to taste with salt and pepper, if using.

4. Spread half the turkey mixture over the base of a shallow baking dish. Spread the macaroni over the turkey. Top with the remaining turkey mixture. Sprinkle with the cheese and bake in the preheated oven for 15–20 minutes until the cheese is golden and bubbling. Serve immediately.

LASAGNE

SERVES: *4* | **PREP:** *20 mins* | **COOK:** *1 hour 15 mins*

INGREDIENTS

2 tbsp olive oil

55 g/2 oz pancetta, chopped

1 onion, chopped

1 garlic clove, finely chopped

225 g/8 oz fresh beef mince

2 celery sticks, chopped

2 carrots, chopped

pinch of sugar

½ tsp dried oregano

400 g/14 oz canned chopped
  tomatoes

2 tsp Dijon mustard

450 ml/16 fl oz ready-made cheese
  sauce

225 g/8 oz no pre-cook lasagne
  sheets

115 g/4 oz freshly grated Parmesan
  cheese

salt and pepper (optional)

1. Preheat the oven to 190°C/375°F/Gas Mark 5. Heat the oil in a large, heavy-based saucepan. Add the pancetta and cook over a medium heat, stirring occasionally, for 3 minutes.

2. Add the onion and garlic and cook, stirring occasionally, for 5 minutes, or until soft.

3. Add the beef and cook, breaking it up with a wooden spoon, until brown all over with no remaining traces of pink. Stir in the celery and carrots and cook for 5 minutes.

4. Season to taste with salt and pepper, if using. Add the sugar, oregano and tomatoes with their can juices. Bring to the boil, then reduce the heat and simmer for 30 minutes.

5. Meanwhile, stir the mustard into the cheese sauce.

6. In a large, rectangular ovenproof dish, make alternate layers of meat sauce, lasagne sheets and cheese.

7. Pour the cheese sauce over the layers, covering them completely, and sprinkle with cheese. Bake in the preheated oven for 30 minutes until golden brown and bubbling. Serve immediately.

SICILIAN
SPAGHETTI CAKE

SERVES: *4* | **PREP:** *25 mins* | **COOK:** *1 hour 15 mins, plus standing*

INGREDIENTS

*125 ml/4 fl oz olive oil, plus extra
  for oiling*

2 aubergines, sliced

350 g/12 oz fresh beef mince

1 onion, chopped

2 garlic cloves, finely chopped

2 tbsp tomato purée

*400 g/14 oz canned chopped
  tomatoes*

1 tsp Worcestershire sauce

*1 tbsp chopped fresh flat-leaf
  parsley*

10 stoned black olives, sliced

*1 red pepper, deseeded and
  chopped*

175 g/6 oz dried spaghetti

*140 g/5 oz freshly grated Parmesan
  cheese*

salt and pepper (optional)

1. Preheat the oven to 200°C/400°F/Gas Mark 6. Brush a 20-cm/ 8-inch loose-based round cake tin with oil and line the base with baking paper. Heat half the oil in a frying pan. Add the aubergines in batches and cook until lightly browned on both sides. Add more oil, as required. Drain the aubergines on kitchen paper, then arrange in overlapping slices to cover the base and side of the prepared tin, reserving a few slices.

2. Heat the remaining oil in a large saucepan and add the beef, onion and garlic. Cook over a medium heat, breaking up the meat with a wooden spoon, until brown. Add the tomato purée, tomatoes and their can juices, Worcestershire sauce and parsley. Season to taste with salt and pepper, if using, and simmer for 10 minutes. Add the olives and red pepper and cook for 10 minutes.

3. Meanwhile, add 1–2 teaspoons of salt, if using, to a large saucepan of water and bring to the boil. Add the pasta, bring back to the boil and cook for 8–10 minutes, or until tender but still firm to the bite. Drain and transfer to a bowl. Add the meat sauce and cheese and toss, then spoon into the cake tin, press down and cover with the remaining aubergine slices. Bake in the preheated oven for 40 minutes. Leave the cake to stand for 5 minutes, then loosen the edges with a knife or spatula and invert onto a plate. Remove and discard the baking paper and serve immediately.

TUNA & BROCCOLI
PASTA BAKE

SERVES: *4* | **PREP:** *15 mins* | **COOK:** *35 mins*

INGREDIENTS

240 g/8½ oz dried wholemeal
  penne pasta
200 g/7 oz broccoli florets
320 g/11 oz canned tuna steak
  in olive oil, drained and
  1½ tablespoons of the oil
  reserved
1 tbsp red pesto
350 g/12 oz passata with onions
  and garlic
6 cherry tomatoes, halved
100 g/3½ oz soft cheese
50 g/1¾ oz Cheddar cheese, grated
25 g/1 oz fresh wholemeal
  breadcrumbs
salt (optional)
200 g/7 oz mixed salad leaves, to
  serve

1. Preheat the oven to 190°C/375°F/Gas Mark 5. Add 1–2 teaspoons of salt, if using, to a large saucepan of water and bring to the boil. Add the pasta, bring back to the boil and cook for 12 minutes, or until tender but still firm to the bite. Drain.

2. Meanwhile, put the broccoli florets into a steamer and steam until just tender. Flake the tuna.

3. Put the reserved tuna oil, the pesto and passata into a saucepan and cook, stirring, over a medium–high heat for 1–2 minutes until warmed through.

4. Tip the cooked pasta into a shallow ovenproof dish along with the sauce, broccoli, tomatoes and tuna. Gently stir until all the pasta is well covered.

5. Dot the top with the soft cheese, then sprinkle over the Cheddar cheese and breadcrumbs. Bake in the preheated oven for 20 minutes, or until heated through and the cheese is golden and melted. Serve immediately with the salad leaves.

RAVIOLI WITH CRABMEAT & RICOTTA

SERVES: *4* | **PREP:** *20–25 mins* | **COOK:** *15 mins*

INGREDIENTS

300 g/10½ oz type 00 pasta flour
1 tsp salt
3 eggs, beaten
70 g/2½ oz butter, melted
salt (optional)

FILLING

175 g/6 oz white crabmeat
175 g/6 oz ricotta cheese
finely grated rind of 1 lemon
¼ tsp dried chilli flakes
2 tbsp chopped fresh flat-leaf
  parsley
salt and pepper (optional)

1. Sift the flour and salt onto a board or work surface, make a well in the centre and add the eggs.

2. Stir with a fork to gradually incorporate the flour into the liquid until a dough forms.

3. Knead the dough for about 5 minutes until smooth. Wrap in clingfilm and leave to rest for 20 minutes.

4. To make the filling, stir together the crabmeat, ricotta cheese, lemon rind, chilli flakes and parsley. Season to taste with salt and pepper, if using.

5. Roll out the dough with a pasta machine or by hand to a thickness of about 3 mm/⅛ inch and cut into 32 x 6-cm/2½-inch squares.

6. Place a spoonful of the filling in the centre of half the squares. Brush the edges with water and place the remaining squares on top, pressing to seal.

7. Add 1–2 teaspoons of salt, if using, to a large saucepan of water and bring to the boil. Add the ravioli, bring back to the boil and cook for 3 minutes, or until tender but still firm to the bite. Drain well.

8. Drizzle the melted butter over the ravioli, sprinkle with pepper, if using, and serve immediately.

MACARONI & SEAFOOD BAKE

SERVES: *4* | **PREP:** *15 mins* | **COOK:** *45 mins*

INGREDIENTS

350 g/12 oz dried macaroni

85 g/3 oz butter, plus extra for greasing

2 small fennel bulbs, trimmed and thinly sliced

175 g/6 oz mushrooms, thinly sliced

175 g/6 oz cooked peeled prawns

pinch of cayenne pepper

600 ml/1 pint béchamel sauce

55 g/2 oz freshly grated Parmesan cheese

2 large tomatoes, halved and sliced

olive oil, for brushing

1 tsp dried oregano

salt (optional)

1. Preheat the oven to 180°C/350°F/Gas Mark 4. Add 1–2 teaspoons of salt, if using, to a large saucepan of water and bring to the boil. Add the pasta, bring back to the boil and cook for 8–10 minutes, or until tender but still firm to the bite.

2. Drain the pasta and return to the pan. Add 25 g/1 oz of the butter, cover, shake the pan and keep warm.

3. Melt the remaining butter in a separate saucepan. Add the fennel and cook for 3–4 minutes. Stir in the mushrooms and cook for a further 2 minutes. Stir in the prawns, then remove the pan from the heat. Stir the cooked pasta, cayenne pepper and prawn mixture into the béchamel sauce.

4. Grease a large ovenproof dish, then pour the mixture into the dish and spread evenly. Sprinkle over the Parmesan cheese and arrange the tomato slices in a ring around the edge. Brush the tomatoes with oil, then sprinkle over the oregano. Bake in the preheated oven for 25 minutes until golden and bubbling. Serve immediately.

SEAFOOD LASAGNE

SERVES: *4* | **PREP:** *20 mins* | **COOK:** *1 hour–1 hour 5 mins, plus standing*

INGREDIENTS

50 g/1¾ oz butter, plus extra for
    greasing
50 g/1¾ oz plain flour
1 tsp mustard powder
600 ml/1 pint milk
2 tbsp olive oil
1 onion, chopped
2 garlic cloves, finely chopped
450 g/1 lb mixed mushrooms, sliced
450 g/1 lb smoked haddock, cut
    into chunks
225 g/8 oz cooked peeled prawns
4–6 no pre-cook lasagne sheets
225 g/8 oz mozzarella cheese,
    chopped
salt and pepper (optional)

1. Preheat the oven to 200°C/400°F/Gas Mark 6. Grease a rectangular ovenproof dish.

2. Melt the butter in a saucepan over a low heat. Add the flour and mustard powder and stir until smooth. Simmer gently for 2 minutes, then gradually add the milk, whisking until smooth. Bring to the boil, reduce the heat and simmer for 2 minutes. Remove from the heat, cover the surface of the white sauce with clingfilm to prevent a skin forming and set aside until needed.

3. Heat the oil in a frying pan over a medium heat. Add the onion and garlic and cook for 5 minutes, or until soft. Add the mushrooms and cook for 5 minutes until soft.

4. Spoon half of the onion, garlic, mushrooms, fish and prawns over the base of the prepared dish and layer half the lasagne sheets over the top. Pour over half the white sauce and sprinkle over half the cheese. Repeat these layers, finishing with sauce and cheese.

5. Bake in the preheated oven for 35–40 minutes, or until golden and the fish is cooked through. Remove from the oven and leave to stand for 10 minutes before serving.

COURGETTE &
RICOTTA LASAGNE

SERVES: *6* | **PREP:** *15 mins* | **COOK:** *1 hour 10 mins*

INGREDIENTS

*3 tbsp olive oil, plus extra for
  brushing*
1 large onion, finely chopped
2 garlic cloves, crushed
500 g/1 lb 2 oz fresh beef mince
2 tbsp tomato purée
*800 g/1 lb 12 oz canned chopped
  tomatoes*
100 ml/3½ fl oz beef stock
*2 tbsp fresh flat-leaf parsley,
  chopped*
400 g/14 oz ricotta cheese
2 eggs, lightly beaten
3 tbsp milk
4 courgettes
*60 g/2¼ oz dried wholemeal
  breadcrumbs*
*40 g/1½ oz freshly grated
  Parmesan cheese*
salt and pepper (optional)

1. Preheat the oven to 180°C/350°F/Gas Mark 4. Heat 1 tablespoon of the oil over a high heat in a medium heavy-based saucepan. Add the chopped onion and fry for 2–3 minutes until just golden. Add the garlic and beef and cook, stirring, for a further 5–6 minutes until brown all over. Stir through the tomato purée, chopped tomatoes and stock, then simmer rapidly for 10–15 minutes until thickened. Stir in the parsley and season to taste with salt and pepper, if using.

2. Meanwhile, place the ricotta cheese in a medium bowl and stir in the eggs. Stir in enough milk to ensure a 'dropping' consistency.

3. Using a sharp knife, slice each courgette lengthways into about 5–6 strips. Brush each strip with a little oil and then fry or griddle until charred and soft.

4. Assemble the lasagne by spreading a layer of the mince mixture over the base of a 1.5-litre/2½-pint ovenproof dish and top with a layer of courgette strips. Sprinkle over the breadcrumbs and spoon over just enough of the ricotta sauce to cover. Repeat to make three layers in total. Finish with the last of the ricotta sauce and the Parmesan. cheese and bake in the preheated oven for 30–35 minutes or until the lasagne is golden brown and bubbling.

INDEX

..... ✗ ....

This edition published by Parragon Books Ltd in 2017
LOVE FOOD is an imprint of Parragon Books Ltd

Parragon Books Ltd
Chartist House
15–17 Trim Street
Bath BA1 1HA, UK
www.parragon.co.uk/love-food
www.parragon.com.au/love-food

ISBN 978-1-4748-6901-0

Printed in China

Introduction by Sarah Bush
Edited by Fiona Biggs
Cover photography by Al Richardson

The cover shot shows the Tagliatelle with Roasted
Pumpkin & Walnut Pesto on page 20.

.... *Notes for the Reader* ....

This book uses both metric and imperial measurements.
Follow the same units of measurement throughout;
do not mix metric and imperial. All spoon measurements
are level: teaspoons are assumed to be 5 ml, and tablespoons
are assumed to be 15 ml. Unless otherwise stated, milk
is assumed to be full fat, eggs and individual fruits and
vegetables are medium, pepper is freshly ground black
pepper and salt is table salt. Unless otherwise stated,
all root vegetables should be peeled prior to using.

The times given are an approximate guide only.
Preparation times differ according to the techniques used
by different people and the cooking times may also vary
from those given.